AMERICA IN THE 1950s

Edmund Lindop

Twenty-First Century Books   Brookfield, Connecticut

For Esther and Laurie, whose steadfast love I cherish

Front cover photographs courtesy of © Bettmann/Corbis (Rosa Parks); National Archives (Nuclear Testing); © Bill Lisenby/Corbis (Juke Box); Dwight D. Eisenhower Library (President Eisenhower); © Bettmann/Corbis (James Dean); Back cover photographs courtesy of Library of Congress (Elvis Presley); © Bettmann/Corbis (Joseph McCarthy)

Photographs courtesy of © TimePix: pp. 1 (A. Y. Owen), 3 (J. R. Eyerman), 13 (Carl Mydans), 35 (Cornell Capa), 44 (Hank Walker), 47 (George Silk), 58 (Michael Rougier), 67 (Joseph Scherschel), 70 (Eliot Elisofon), 75 (A. Y. Owen), 85 (Bill Bridges), 87 (Gordon Tenney/Black Star), 88 (J. R. Eyerman), 91 (Lisa Larsen), 96 (Robert W. Kelley), 109 (Herb Scharfman); AP/Wide World Photos: pp. 4, 21, 25, 39, 53 (left), 62, 71, 79, 102, 105; © Bettmann/Corbis: p. 53 (right); Underwood Photo Archives, S.F.: p. 69; Brown Brothers: p. 101

Library of Congress Cataloging-in-Publication Data
Lindop, Edmund.
America in the 1950s / Edmund Lindop.
p. cm.
Includes bibliographical references and index.
Contents: The Korean War — A Red scare haunts Americans — "I Like Ike" and "I'm Madly for Adlai" — African Americans seek racial justice — The Cold War escalates — Big changes come to the United States — Television takes center stage — More entertainment — A golden age of sports.
Summary: Outlines life in the United States in the 1950s, including the development of suburbia, advances in technology and entertainment, politics, the space race, and the Cold War.
ISBN 0-7613-2551-4 (lib. bdg.)
1. United States—Civilization—1945—-Juvenile literature. 2. United States—History—1945-1953—Juvenile literature. 3. United States—History—1953-1961—Juvenile literature. 4. Nineteen fifties—Juvenile literature. [1. United States—Civilization—1945- 2. United States—History—1945-1953. 3. United States—History—1953-1961. 4. Nineteen fifties.] I. Title.
E169.12 .L546 2002   973.921—dc21   2001052254

Published by Twenty-First Century Books
A Division of The Millbrook Press, Inc.
2 Old New Milford Road
Brookfield, Connecticut 06804
www.millbrookpress.com

CONTENTS

The United States first tested a hydrogen bomb in the Marshall Islands in the Pacific on November 1, 1952. Far more powerful than the devastating atomic bombs that had been dropped on Japan seven years earlier, the hydrogen bomb was a grim introduction to the Cold War era.

This book is about the 1950s, a decade that began more than half a century ago. It was one of the most significant periods in the history of the United States, mainly because it ushered in many changes that still affect our lives today.

The development of the hydrogen bomb in the 1950s, which accelerated the Cold War between the United States and the Soviet Union, remains a constant threat. The hydrogen bomb could now be used by many countries that did not possess it in the 1950s. The "space race" that was initiated in that decade not only led to the first walk on the moon and satellites in outer space, but also to remarkable new developments in computer technology and medicine.

Vast changes in lifestyle that began in the fifties have continued and expanded. Some of the most important sprang from the advent of television, the move of people from inner cities to growing suburbs, increased economic productivity, and an extension of civil rights to minorities, especially African Americans, which has fostered the democratic principles on which our country's greatness depends.

In the 1930s, Americans were plagued by the Great Depression, and from 1941 to 1945, they endured the devastating effects of World War II. When the Japanese government officially surrendered on September 2, 1945, people throughout the world celebrated. World War II, which cost millions of lives, left other millions seriously injured, and destroyed huge amounts of property, was finally over! The Grand Alliance, consisting of the United States, Great Britain, France, and the Soviet Union, had vanquished Adolf Hitler's Germany, Benito Mussolini's Italy, and the warlords of imperial Japan.

The prospects for a lasting peace appeared very bright. To help preserve this cherished peace, the United Nations (UN) had been established in 1945. It included most of the world's nations and supplanted the League of Nations, which had been established at the end of World War I.

The United States hastily demobilized most of its armed forces. Millions of American men and women were freed from military duty and joyfully returned to their families. "No people in history have been known to disengage themselves so quickly from the ways of war," commented President Harry S. Truman.[1] By early 1947, American armed forces had been cut from their wartime strength of 12 million to 1.5 million, and the annual military budget had dropped from $90.9 billion to $10.3 billion.

The Soviet Union, however, did not dismantle its mighty war machine. It kept intact its huge army, thousands of military airplanes, and a large armada of fighting ships. This was because the Soviets planned to extend Communist rule over vast areas.

Even before World War II ended, the Soviet Union had gobbled up three small independent countries that faced the Baltic Sea—Estonia, Latvia, and Lithuania. Following the war,

"No people in history have been known to disengage themselves so quickly from the ways of war."

it broke its promise to permit free elections in Poland and other countried in Eastern Europe. Instead, it turned these nations into Communist "puppet" states. In 1946, former British Prime Minister Winston Churchill solemnly declared that an "Iron Curtain has descended" to cut off from the world the Russian-controlled countries in Eastern Europe."[2]

When the Soviet Union attempted to extend its rule over Greece and Turkey in 1947, President Truman and the U.S. Congress quickly furnished military and economic assistance that prevented a Communist takeover of these countries. Also in 1947, the United States launched the Marshall Plan to help Europe recover economically from the ravages of World War II. The plan provided $13 billion in loans to sixteen countries, some of which were so poor that they might have otherwise turned to communism. The Soviet Union was offered this plan, but it turned down American assistance.

Defeated Germany, for example, was the scene of a serious postwar problem. The United States, Great Britain, France, and the Soviet Union each were originally assigned one zone to govern until a peace treaty could be signed to reunite Germany. The Russians, however, refused to permit their zone to be merged with the other zones. Consequently, Germany remained divided. Eventually it became two separate nations—West Germany, which was democratic, and East Germany, which continued under Communist rule.

Berlin, Germany's largest city, lay 110 miles (177 kilometers) inside East Germany. It was divided into two sections, Communist East Berlin and independent West Berlin. An ominous threat occurred in 1948 when the Communists shut down all the highways, railroads, and water routes that ran from West Berlin to West Germany. By cutting off all trade links between isolated West Berlin and West Germany, the Communists believed that when the West Berliners no longer received food and fuel from West Germany they would be forced to surrender their freedom.

President Truman, however, was determined that West Berlin would not be absorbed by the Communists. In June 1948, he ordered a massive airlift in which large numbers of airplanes would fly food, fuel, and other supplies to West Berlin. This was a dangerous move, since the Communists might have attacked the planes, perhaps starting World War III. But the Communists did not interfere with the flights, and many months later they ended their siege of West Berlin.

In 1949, the North Atlantic Treaty Organization (NATO) was formed. It provided a military alliance originally of twelve nations and later sixteen that pledged joint action in case of a Communist attack against any member nation. The United States took the lead in proposing NATO, and General Dwight D. Eisenhower was its first military commander.

A trouble spot in another part of the world was China. After a lengthy civil war, in 1949 the Communist forces headed by Mao Tse-tung conquered the non-Communist government run by Chiang Kai-shek and forced Chiang's followers to flee to the island of Formosa (Taiwan). China then became an ally of the Soviet Union in promoting the Communist cause.

Despite the deteriorating relations between the free world and the Communist powers, most Americans felt reasonably secure because they alone had atomic bombs, and surely no country would dare attack them or their allies and risk possible annihilation. Then, on September 23, 1949, President Truman grimly announced that the Soviet Union had exploded an atomic device. This shocking revelation instantly and dramatically altered the perception of a permanent peace. Republican Senator Arthur Vandenberg ominously declared that this "is now a different world," and Democratic Senator Tom Connally added, "Russia has shown her teeth."[3]

A Gallup poll taken in 1950 showed that 41 percent of Americans felt their country would fight another war within five years, 75 percent believed that cities in the United States would be bombed in the next war, and 19 percent feared that this war, when it came, would destroy the entire human race.

Only five years after World War II ended, the Cold War had taken center stage, and it would frighten people throughout the world for nearly half a century.

ONE

The Korean War

During the final weeks of World War II, both American and Soviet troops moved in to occupy Korea, which had been annexed by Japan in 1910. Americans held the southern part of this peninsula east of China, and the Soviets took over the northern part. This followed an agreement made at the Yalta Conference in 1945 permitting Soviet and American armed forces to occupy Korea, with a demarcation line along the thirty-eighth parallel of latitude, until the establishment of a postwar unified and independent Korean government.

The plan to establish a united Korea did not meet with success. Separate governments were established in anti-Communist South Korea and Communist North Korea. These new nations were eager to absorb each other. UN attempts to hold all-Korean elections to set up a unified state were turned down by the Soviet Union.

At first, the United States showed little interest in defending South Korea against possible aggression from North Korea. In June 1949, the last American troops were removed from South Korea. Then, in January 1950, U.S. Secretary of State Dean Acheson announced what was in effect a new American policy in the Far East. The United States would protect a defensive perimeter that ran from the Aleutian Islands off the coast of Alaska to Japan and the Philippines. But aggression outside this perimeter—including Korea—would have to be met by the peoples involved or by the UN.

NORTH KOREA INVADES SOUTH KOREA

June 25, 1950, dawned as an ordinary day for most Americans. President Truman had gone home to Independence, Missouri, to enjoy a family reunion, and many top officials in the U.S. government were on vacation.

At 9:26 A.M., the State Department received a startling cable from John Muccio, the American ambassador in Seoul, the capital of South Korea. It read: "North Korean forces invaded the Republic of Korea at several places this morning. . . . It would appear from the nature of the attack and the manner in which it was launched that it constitutes an all-out offensive against the Republic of Korea."[1]

When President Truman received this ominous message, he flew back quickly to Washington, D.C. He knew that the South Koreans were facing an aggressor that had an enormous advantage. North Korea's armed forces totaled 150,000 men, of which 89,000 were trained combat troops. Although the Russians had removed their troops, they left behind a large amount of equipment, including mortars, howitzers, antitank guns, 150 tanks, plus some MIG fighting airplanes.

"North Korean

forces invaded

the Republic

of Korea this

morning."

Against this formidable foe, the South Koreans had only 65,000 troops. Just one regiment of their four divisions was near the border in defensive position, and more than a third of these troops were helping with the harvest. The South Koreans were poorly armed. They had old Japanese-model rifles, short-range howitzers, small mortars, obsolete bazookas, no offensive artillery, no tanks, and no warplanes.

The North Koreans were supremely confident that they could win a complete victory over their weaker adversaries. The chief of operations, General Yu Suncheol, told his officers that their army had so far conducted only minor combat operations. "But now all divisions will be unified in a major maneuver. It will be the largest and most significant one since the inauguration of our Korea People's Army, and as such it calls for perfection."[2] General Yu said that this all-out attack was a top-secret matter and should not be discussed with anyone.

On his three-hour trip back to the White House, President Truman compared the past to the present situation. "I remembered how each time that the democracies failed to act it had encouraged the aggressors to keep going ahead. Communism was acting in Korea just as Hitler, Mussolini, and the Japanese had acted ten, fifteen, and twenty years earlier. . . . If this [Korean war] was allowed to go unchallenged, it would mean a third world war. . . . It was also clear to me that the foundations and the principles of the United Nations were at stake unless this unprovoked attack on Korea could be stopped."[3]

When Trygve Lie, the first secretary-general of the UN, heard about the invasion, he declared, "This is war against the United States."[4] And so it was. The two Koreas were wards of the UN, and the United States represented it in South Korea.

Members of the UN Security Council hastily assembled in an emergency meeting. They voted that the UN would take up arms to end North Korean aggression. The Soviet Union could have vetoed this resolution, but its delegate was not present. Six months earlier, the Soviet delegate had walked out when the Security Council had refused to admit Communist China to the UN, and he still was absent. This made it possible for the new world organization to vote that its member nations would strike back against a country that had broken the peace.

The North Korean government did not respond to the UN resolution, so two days later a follow-up resolution provided that "the members of the United Nations furnish such assistance to the Republic of Korea as may be necessary to repel the armed attack and to restore international peace and security in the area."[5] Then the Security Council designated the United States as its chief agent for pursuing the war in Korea.

Besides the United States, fifteen other nations sent military forces to South Korea that eventually numbered about 19,000 troops. Forty-one other countries sent money, food, clothing, and medical supplies. But most of the fighting was done by men from the United States and South Korea.

President Truman named General Douglas MacArthur as commander of the UN armed forces in Korea. During World War II, MacArthur had led the American campaign in the Pacific Ocean area, and after the war he was the supreme commander of the occupation forces in Japan, where he helped establish a constitutional monarchy.

General MacArthur faced a very difficult task in defending South Korea. The fast-moving North Koreans nearly won the war in its first few weeks. They captured the South Korean capital of Seoul and quickly pressed forward until they almost reached the port of Pusan at the southern tip of the peninsula.

At first, MacArthur's forces consisted of only four undermanned and partially trained U.S. Army divisions and the badly outnumbered South Korean troops. But soon the U.S. Joint Chiefs of Staff sent large numbers of additional soldiers, marines, and air and naval forces to South Korea. With this large number of reinforcements, UN forces stiffened and held firm. They were able to stabilize their position along the Naktong River near Pusan.

Meanwhile, General MacArthur began planning a daring amphibious landing far to the north of Pusan. He selected the port of Inchon, despite its high tides and swift currents. MacArthur knew that the North Koreans, concentrated in the south, would be vulnerable to an invasion so far to the north. He believed the capture of Inchon would lead quickly to the conquest of Seoul, the hub of the country's chief roads and railroads that connected the capital city to the southern region.

On September 15, 1950, U.S. marines successfully assaulted Inchon, and they were followed by a large contingent of army troops. Two weeks later Seoul fell, and by October 1, the UN forces held a line near the thirty-eighth parallel. Under heavy fire, the North Korean soldiers had to scurry back to their own country.

South Korea again was a free and independent nation.

General Douglas MacArthur roars an order from the U.S.S. Mount McKinley at the landing at Inchon on September 15, 1950.

THE UN COUNTERATTACK PROVOKES A NEW, DANGEROUS FOE

What would happen next? Would the UN forces be content to liberate South Korea and quit fighting? Or would they attempt to move north of the thirty-eighth parallel and try to unify the two Koreas?

Initially, President Truman said that the U.S. National Security Council had studied the matter and recommended against crossing the thirty-eighth parallel because removing the aggressors from South Korea was a sufficient victory. General MacArthur, however, insisted that his troops be permitted to invade the north, and if this happened, he predicted that all of Korea would be united by Thanksgiving.

The Joint Chiefs of Staff urged that MacArthur be cautious because ominous rumblings were being heard from Communist China. It was reported that many Chinese divisions were massing in Manchuria, just across the Yalu River from North Korea, but these reports could not be confirmed.

President Truman believed that it was time to confer with General MacArthur. He flew to Wake Island, where the two men met on October 15. Truman asked about the chance of either Chinese or Russian intervention if the war was extended to North Korea.

The general replied that there was "very little" chance that these large Communist countries would be drawn into the war. "Had they interfered in the first or second months it would have been decisive. We are no longer fearful of their intervention. We no longer stand hat in hand. . . . Now that we have bases for our Air Force in Korea, if the Chinese tried to get down to Pyongyang [North Korea's capital], there would be the greatest slaughter."[6]

The UN General Assembly passed a resolution calling for the unification of Korea, and this gave MacArthur the authority he needed to send his forces northward. There still was concern about possible Chinese or Russian intervention. The Chinese foreign minister informed the Indian ambassador in Peking that if the UN armies crossed the thirty-eighth parallel, "China would send troops to the Korean frontier to defend North Korea."[7] MacArthur believed the Chinese were bluffing.

UN forces pushed triumphantly through most of North Korea. Pyongyang and the east coast port of Wonsan were captured easily in October. Just as it appeared that North Korean resistance had completely collapsed, advanced American troops encountered huge Chinese units 50 miles (80 km) south of the Yalu River. By November 2, U.S. intelligence officers had accumulated evidence that China had massed about 850,000 troops in its Manchurian province and had secretly moved the first divisions across the Yalu River into North Korea on October 19. MacArthur's assessment of Chinese intentions was entirely wrong.

As thousands of Chinese soldiers stormed into North Korea, a disaster of huge proportions began taking shape. The 2nd Infantry Division tried desperately to halt the Chinese advance. But in the final few days of November, the 2nd Division suffered five thousand casualties, or roughly one-third of its men.

MacArthur

———

believed the

———

Chinese were

———

bluffing.

On November 30, as the UN forces were swiftly retreating, at a White House press conference a reporter asked Truman whether he might use the atomic bomb in the war. The deeply troubled president replied, "There has always been active consideration of its use."[8] Truman knew that such action would trigger World War III, which he strongly wanted to avoid if there was any other possible solution.

The Chinese armies, bolstered by revitalized North Korean troops, pushed relentlessly southward. Finally they reached the thirty-eighth parallel where the war had begun.

PRESIDENT TRUMAN FIRES GENERAL MACARTHUR

General MacArthur persisted in his demand that there is no "substitute for victory." To accomplish this goal, he called for bombing military and industrial sites on the Chinese side of the Yalu River, a naval blockade of China's coasts, and unleashing Chiang Kai-shek's Nationalist troops in Formosa to invade the Chinese mainland.

The bellicose general sent these ideas to Congressman Joseph Martin, the Republican minority leader of the House of Representatives. When Martin released this letter to the press, President Truman felt that he had to remove General MacArthur from his command.

The president solemnly declared,

> I believe we must try to limit the war to Korea for these vital reasons: to make sure that the precious lives of our fighting men are not wasted; to see that the security of our country and the free world is not needlessly jeopardized; and to prevent a third world war. A number of events have made it evident that General MacArthur did not agree with that policy. I have therefore considered it essential to relieve General MacArthur so that there would be no doubt or confusion as to the real purpose and aim of our policy.[9]

When MacArthur was officially fired on April 11, 1951, he was replaced by General Matthew Ridgway as commander of the UN forces in Korea. The dismissal of MacArthur unleashed one of the hottest controversies of the entire decade.

Truman's supporters felt he had acted correctly as the nation's commander in chief. Editorial writers for such prominent newspapers as the *New York Times, Washington Post,* and *Christian Science Monitor* agreed with the president. Speaker of the House Sam Rayburn said, "We must never give up that the military is subject to and under control of the civilian administration." Eleanor Roosevelt said, "I do not think that a general should make policy." General Omar Bradley, chairman of the Joint Chiefs of Staff, later stated that MacArthur's "strategy would involve us in the wrong war, at the wrong place, at the wrong time and with the wrong enemy."[10]

The president's opponents, chiefly Republicans who felt that his administration had been "soft on Communists," lashed out bitterly at his decision to fire MacArthur. Thomas E. Dewey, governor of New York and twice the Republican candidate for the presidency, said that Truman's dismissal of MacArthur "is the culmination of disastrous failure of leadership in Washington." Senator Richard M. Nixon of California cried out, "President Truman has given [the Communists] just what they were after—MacArthur's scalp." Senator William Jenner of Indiana even went so far as to state, "Our only choice is to impeach President Truman."[11]

Huge crowds hailed MacArthur as a mistreated hero on his return to the United States. In San Francisco, the trip from the airport to his hotel took two hours because thousands of wildly enthusiastic supporters lined the streets.

Two days later, on April 19, MacArthur delivered an impassioned speech to Congress, which was watched on television by an estimated 20 million viewers. He maintained that the free world could not surrender to Communists in Asia, and again claimed that there is "no substitute for victory."

His concluding remarks were so dramatic that they were remembered for decades by people who heard them:

Huge crowds hailed MacArthur as a mistreated hero.

This world has turned over many times since I took the oath on the plain at West Point, and the hopes and dreams have long since vanished, but I still remember the refrain of one of the most popular barracks ballads of that day which proclaimed most proudly that old soldiers never die; they just fade away. And like the old soldier of that ballad, I now close my military career and just fade away, an old soldier who tried to do his duty as God gave him the light to see that duty. Good-bye.[12]

A STALEMATE FINALLY LEADS TO PEACE

By mid-June 1951, the UN forces had stopped the North Korean advance near the thirty-eighth parallel. A short time later, the Chinese and North Koreans agreed to meet UN representatives at Panmunjom, a town between the two lines, to begin negotiating a peace treaty. But the negotiations dragged on, month after month.

Meanwhile, sporadic fighting continued. The war entered a new phase defined by elevated sites called Heartbreak Ridge, Pork Chop Hill, Punchbowl, Sniper's Ridge, and other hilltops located between the two armies. At these high places violent battles occurred, as each side tried desperately to gain a little more ground.

The most difficult issue to resolve at the negotiating table was what to do about the prisoners of war (POWs). The Communists insisted at first on forced repatriation, but it appeared that many Communist prisoners did not want to return home. The International Red Cross polled these men held by the UN armies. The startling results, announced in April 1952, showed that of 132,000 Chinese and North Korean prisoners polled, only 54,000 North Koreans and 5,100 Chinese wanted to be sent home. This was a staggering blow to Communist pride and greatly stalled the negotiations.

A whole year passed before the talks resumed at Panmunjom. There, a final solution to the POW problem was resolved. A neutral commission was established to interview the prisoners. If they still did not want to be forced back home, the commission was empowered to release them to whichever country they chose.

On July 27, 1953, the peace treaty was finally signed. The human losses in the Korean War were enormous. Chinese and North Korean casualties were not announced, but estimates of their total losses amounted to nearly 2 million armed men plus about another million civilians. Total casualties for the UN forces (killed, wounded, and missing) were 459,300, of whom more than 250,000 were South Koreans. Of the 1.8 million Americans who served in Korea, 54,200 were killed, 103,300 were wounded, and 8,200 were missing in action.

Nevertheless, some major accomplishments resulted from the Korean War. It caused the United States to arm itself on a permanent basis and to keep its military forces at a high state of combat readiness. Never in the future would the United States be as poorly prepared to resist aggression as it was when the Korean War began. The Korean hostilities prompted the United States to strengthen its military commitment to NATO and to create in 1954 the Southeast Asia Treaty Organization (SEATO), providing collective action if member nations in Southeast Asia were attacked.

The Korean War ended U.S. discrimination against African-American soldiers, who had to fight in segregated divisions in World War I and World War II. President Truman ordered integration firmly established in Korea. Black and white servicepeople now fought side by side, ate in the same mess halls, and slept in the same barracks.

While neither side was fully victorious, the Korean War demonstrated that through the collective action of the UN an aggressor could be prevented from conquering another country, and without the use of dreaded atomic weapons.

TWO

A Red Scare Haunts Americans

Many bewildered Americans wondered how the Russians could have launched an atomic explosion as early as 1949. Would this have been possible without widespread spying and espionage?

A wrenching feeling of hysteria was gripping the country. President Truman had contributed to this hysteria by launching a massive security program in 1947. Between then and 1952, about 6.6 million government employees were investigated. Not a single case of espionage was uncovered, but about five hundred persons were dismissed because of "questionable loyalty." Despite the failure to find subversion, the broad scope of this "Red hunt" caused many people to fear that the government was riddled with spies.

Richard M. Nixon, a young congressman from California, was suddenly catapulted into fame as a national hero when he led the tough questioning by the House Un-American Activities Committee (HUAC) of Alger Hiss, a former State Department official. Whittaker Chambers, a self-confessed former Communist spy, said that in the 1930s, Hiss had given him secret government documents that Chambers microfilmed and hid in a pumpkin on his Maryland farm. Chambers turned over these documents to the HUAC, but Hiss denied the charges under oath.

On January 21, 1950, Hiss was convicted of perjury following two of the most highly publicized trials in American history. Although Hiss could not be tried for espionage because the statute of limitations had expired, his conviction of perjury led to a five-year prison sentence. The Hiss case, Nixon declared, was only "a small part of the whole shocking story of Communist espionage in the United States."[1]

Two weeks after Hiss had been found guilty, the British government announced the arrest of Dr. Klaus Fuchs, a high-level scientist who had worked on the development of the atom bomb at Los Alamos, New Mexico, during World War II. Fuchs confessed to having spied for the Soviet Union and giving that country top-secret information on how to build the bomb.

Investigators linked Fuchs to Americans Harry Gold, Morton Sobel, and Julius and Ethel Rosenberg. Gold and Sobel were convicted and given long prison terms.

The evidence against the Rosenbergs came largely from Ethel Rosenberg's brother, David Greenglass, who had been part of the wartime spy network. When the FBI interrogated Julius Rosenberg, he refused to give information about his spying or to name any other agents. At their trial, the Rosenbergs continued their silence. The jury convicted the Rosenbergs of espionage, and Judge Irving Kaufman sentenced both of them to the electric chair. The judge rebuked the Rosenbergs' "diabolical conspiracy to destroy a God-fearing nation" and claimed that the secrets they had revealed to the Soviets gave Russia the atomic bomb "years before our best scientists had predicted."[2]

Ethel and Julius Rosenberg were photographed as they rode to separate jails in New York City on March 29, 1951, after they were convicted of espionage. They were executed two years later.

A lengthy appeal process brought requests for clemency by some prominent persons, including Albert Einstein and Pope Pius XII. But on June 9, 1953, the Rosenbergs were executed and became the first native-born Americans to be put to death for espionage by order of a civilian court.

REDS UNDER THE BEDS

One evening in 1950, a couple in Houston, Texas, entered a Chinese restaurant and conversed with the proprietor about producing a radio program covering recent Chinese history. Overhearing their conversation, a nearby man phoned the police and told them that the people were "talking communism."[3] The couple were immediately arrested and jailed for fourteen hours before the police concluded that there was no evidence of espionage.

Such extreme behavior was very common during the so-called Red Scare. A Hollywood studio canceled a film about Hiawatha because she had tried to end wars between Indian tribes, and movie audiences might see this as propaganda for a possible Communist peace offensive. A foundation offered $100,000 for research that could create a device for detecting traitors. The U.S. Immigration Service, in an effort to prove that an alien was a Communist, had a witness testify that this man preferred soccer, a game often played in foreign countries, to football. "What an insult to this country," the witness haughtily declared.[4]

In a 1954 national survey, more than half of the people interviewed said that all known Communists should be jailed, and 78 percent thought Americans should report to the FBI neighbors or acquaintances whom they suspected of being Communists.

Many states, cities, and counties imposed loyalty oaths on teachers and college professors. So did some corporations and labor unions. These targeted people had to swear their allegiance to the United States and deny that they ever had any

People had to swear their allegiance to the United States and deny that they ever had any Communist affiliations.

Communist affiliations. Conservatives sometimes used these loyalty oaths to chastise individuals who were not Communists but merely liberals, radical labor leaders, civil rights activists, or pacifists.

About 250 Hollywood personalities were blacklisted and denied future work during the purge of the early 1950s because they were labeled former or present-day Communists. This purge also spread to Broadway and the music industry. Among the best-known blacklisted individuals were actors Jose Ferrer, Will Geer, Lee J. Cobb, Edward G. Robinson, and actor-director Orson Welles; writers Arthur Miller, Lillian Hellman, Dashiell Hammett, Langston Hughes, Ring Lardner Jr., and Dalton Trumbo; singers Paul Robeson, Lena Horne, and Pete Seeger; composer Aaron Copland; and composer-conductor Leonard Bernstein. For example, Miller and Hellman were accused of writing plays that contained "subversive" ideas; and Robeson was charged with having Communist contacts.

Some of these blacklisted persons were given no work in the United States for many years. A few went into exile in Great Britain or other foreign countries. Charlie Chaplin, who was living in Britain but had resided in the United States for nearly thirty years, refused to return to America because he knew he would face questions of a political nature from an immigration board. One of the blacklisted individuals, Dalton Trumbo, cleverly decided to use a pseudonym and won an Academy Award in 1956 for a screenplay written under the name Robert Rich.

The media rushed to turn out many tales with strongly anti-Communist themes. Hollywood produced such films as *I Married a Communist*, *The Iron Curtain*, *The Red Menace*, and *I Was a Communist for the FBI*. Bookstores carried such titles as *The Red Plotters*, *The Soviet Spies*, and *I Chose Freedom*. Herbert Philbrick's story about how he had been a Communist and became an FBI informer, *I Led Three Lives*, was serialized in about five hundred newspapers and adapted into a television series.

America's obsession with ferreting out Communists attracted the attention of Mickey Spillane, one of the decade's most popular writers. Instead of Spillane's central character, Mike Hammer, chasing gangsters and corrupt politicians, he began pursuing suspected subversives. In Spillane's 1951 thriller, *One Lonely Night,* Hammer brags, "I killed more people tonight than I have fingers on my hands. I shot them in cold blood and enjoyed every minute of it. . . . They were Commies. . . .They never thought there were people like me in this country. They figured us all to be soft as horse manure and just as stupid."[5]

McCARTHY CRUSADES AGAINST U.S. COMMUNISTS

Joseph McCarthy gave himself the gutsy nickname of "Tail-gunner Joe," although during World War II most of his time was spent serving as an intelligence officer and doing paperwork for a squadron of pilots. Elected a U.S. senator from Wisconsin in 1946, he was a slightly known, almost inconspicuous member of Congress during the first four years of his term.

With his contest for reelection looming in two years, McCarthy was desperate to find some issue that would bring him a huge amount of favorable publicity. Finally he decided to become a major spokesman in the mounting campaign to expose Communists in the United States. He was especially eager to pursue those in the government, which he claimed "is full of Communists. The thing to do is to hammer at them."[6]

McCarthy first drew national attention with a sensational speech before a women's Republican club in Wheeling, West Virginia, on February 9, 1950. "I have here in my hand," he declared, waving a sheaf of papers, "a list of 205 names known to the secretary of state as being members of the Communist Party and who nevertheless are still working and shaping the policy of the State Department."[7]

Senator Joseph McCarthy points to a map labeled "Communist Party Organization, U.S.A., Feb. 9, 1950" during testimony in June 1954, six months before he was censured by the Senate.

The senator told the club that the reason the United States found itself in a weak position in international affairs "is not because our only powerful potential enemy has sent men to invade our shores, but rather because of the traitorous actions of those who have been treated so well by this Nation."[8]

When later asked to produce his list of 205 Communists in the State Department, McCarthy said he could not find it. In a subsequent speech, he reduced the number to 57, but again he did not identify any of those whom he accused.

Finally, under protection of senatorial immunity, McCarthy began to name some of his targets. He called Secretary of State Dean Acheson "The Red Dean" and charged that U.S. ambassador to the United Nations, Philip Jessup, was "preaching the Communist line." He even attacked highly respected General George Marshall, head of the American armed forces in World War II and later secretary of state, as "a man steeped in falsehood" and "an instrument of the Soviet conspiracy."[9]

McCarthy claimed that Far East expert Owen Lattimore was the top Russian espionage agent in the United States. Lattimore later was cleared of any pro-Communist leanings. He called McCarthy "a madman" and reminded reporters "that [McCarthy's] writings had been condemned by Soviet, Chinese Communist, and Mongolian critics."[10]

Besides name-calling, McCarthy quickly proved that he could destroy people's political careers. Senator Millard Tydings, a conservative Maryland Democrat, chaired a 1950 Senate subcommittee that declared that McCarthy's charges against the State Department were a hoax. Tydings ran for reelection later that year, and McCarthy was determined to get revenge. He had a composite photograph put together that falsely showed Tydings talking amiably with Earl Browder, the former head of the U.S. Communist Party. Then he saturated Maryland voters with copies of this fake photograph, which was widely believed to have been the chief reason Tydings was defeated for a fifth Senate term. McCarthy also attacked other senators who opposed him and helped to defeat Senate Democratic floor leader Scott Lucas of Illinois, Ernest MacFarland of Arizona, and Raymond Baldwin and William Benton of Connecticut.

Despite his failure to provide any proof against the individuals he assailed, McCarthy had many followers who approved of his campaign against American Communists. *Newsweek* interpreted the figures of a Gallup poll conducted on May 21, 1950, as showing that 46.4 percent of those interviewed thought that McCarthy was doing "a good thing for the country"; only 34.5 percent thought he was not, and 19.1 percent had no opinion. Even Senator Robert Taft of Illinois, the most powerful and widely respected Republican in Congress, said that "the pro-Communist policies of the State Department fully justified Joe McCarthy in his demand for an investigation."[11]

"Tail-gunner Joe" easily won reelection to the Senate in 1952.

McCarthy's Bombast is Finally Silenced

The Wisconsin senator's popularity continued to rise until he began an investigation of the U.S. Army in October 1953. The subject was supposed subversion at Fort Monmouth Army Signal Corps Center. Unable to prove any espionage there, in January 1954 he attacked the routine promotion at Camp Kilmer of a liberal captain, Irving Peress. McCarthy thundered at Camp Kilmer's commander, General Ralph Zwicker, a World War II combat hero, "You are a disgrace to the uniform. You're not fit to be an officer. You're ignorant."[12]

Millions of Americans sat glued to their television sets, enthralled by the war between McCarthy and the army. The confrontation began turning against McCarthy when it was revealed that the army had drafted G. David Schine, a member of McCarthy's staff, and that Roy Cohn, McCarthy's chief counsel, had tried repeatedly and unsuccessfully to force the army to raise Schine's rank from private to lieutenant.

The counsel for the army was Joseph Welch, a usually soft-spoken lawyer who had a bright mind and shrewd insight. When he questioned Cohn about Communists supposedly flourishing at Fort Monmouth, Cohn pleaded that he had a poor memory and could not remember anything about that situation.

Then McCarthy furiously assailed Fred Fisher, a lawyer who worked for Welch's firm. When the Wisconsin senator relentlessly reviled Fisher for no reason except that he once had been a member of the National Lawyer's Guild, a liberal organization, Welch struck back. "Until this moment, Senator," he declared, "I think I never really gauged your cruelty or your recklessness. Fred Fisher is starting what looks to be a brilliant career with us. Little did I dream you could be so reckless and so cruel as to do an injury to that lad. I fear he shall always bear a scar needlessly inflicted by you. . . . You have done enough. Have you no sense of decency, sir, at long last? Have you left no sense of decency?"[13]

"Have you no sense of decency, sir, at long last? Have you left no sense of decency?"

For the first time, a large part of the American public saw McCarthy as a mean-spirited, lying brute who had damaged the careers of many innocent people. His glory faded quickly.

On December 2, 1954, the Senate, including many Republicans, took strong action against McCarthy. It censured him by a vote of 67 to 22.

McCarthy strode for two more years through the Senate corridors, but he was a gloomy man. His despair grew worse, and he started staying home rather than going to his office. Day after day he would watch TV soap operas while staring into the fireplace. Always a heavy drinker, he developed cirrhosis of the liver. The fallen senator died in 1957 at the age of forty-eight.

The term "McCarthyism" lived on. For some, it described the leading figure of the anti-Communist furor. For others, it pointed with shame at the senator's outrageous political style of reckless accusation and character assassination.

THREE

"I Like Ike" and "I'm Madly for Adlai"

For twenty years, since the election of Franklin D. Roosevelt in 1932, the White House had been occupied by Democrats Roosevelt and Harry S. Truman. In 1948, the Republicans thought they had a sure winner in New York governor Thomas E. Dewey, but Truman defeated him in the most stunning upset in American political history.

In 1952, the Republicans felt supremely confident that they could finally regain the presidency. They had a powerful, three-pronged formula for success: The Korean War, corruption, and communism. The Korean War was then in a lengthy stalemate, and Republicans charged that the Truman administration had denied General MacArthur and his military forces the means to win it. Corruption was prevalent in Washington, D.C., and some of Truman's closest cronies had done favors for their friends and received in return money, a freezer for preserving food, and a mink coat. Joseph McCarthy was still riding high in 1952, and Republicans insisted that the Democrats had been coddling Communists in the national government for many years. Americans also were suffering from higher consumer prices, heavier tax burdens, little increase in wages, and labor unrest.

"Had enough?" Republicans asked the American public. They solemnly promised to "clean up the horrible mess in Washington." Their only challenge was to run a candidate for the presidency who was sufficiently attractive to win the election in a nation that still had a majority of voters who called themselves Democrats or Independents.

REPUBLICANS SELECT THEIR PRESIDENTIAL NOMINEE

Senator Robert A. Taft announced in September 1951 that he was running for president. The son of former president William Howard Taft, he crisscrossed the country on a quest for convention delegates during the first half of 1952. Known widely as "Mr. Republican," he was clearly the choice of the party's conservative wing. The sparse-haired, bespectacled senator with a dry, metallic voice was not a rousing speaker, but his intelligence, hard work, and consistent partisanship caused his supporters to overlook his lack of charisma and personal warmth.

Some Republicans, however, wondered whether Taft could win the election. They knew that many Independents and most Democrats probably would not vote for a man who had been an isolationist, a defender of McCarthy, a critic of organized labor, and an extreme conservative. They sought someone who would have more widespread popular appeal.

In the wings was a man who could supply what Taft lacked in popularity. General Dwight D. "Ike" Eisenhower was a beloved hero who had led the World War II allied armies in Europe to victory before he became commander of the NATO forces. Still, no one knew whether Ike, who had never held a political office, would run for the presidency, or even if he was a Republican.

In 1948, both the Republicans and the Democrats had tried to get Eisenhower to head their ticket. But he had flatly turned down their offers.

When efforts were being made to pull him into the political arena for the 1952 election, Eisenhower's reservations remained, and he told his brother Milton that he had no intention of "voluntarily abandoning this critical duty [NATO] unless I reach a conviction that an even larger *duty* compels me to do so." "Anybody is a damn fool if he actually seeks to be president," he told friends. "Some people think there is a lot of power and glory attached to the job. On the contrary, the very workings of a democratic system see to it that the job has very little power."[1]

Nevertheless, the pressure on Ike to become a presidential candidate mounted steadily. In early January 1952, he gave his permission to enter his name in the New Hampshire primary election, and on January 27, he finally announced that he was a Republican. Running in New Hampshire was an effort to test his appeal, and Eisenhower remained in Europe and did no campaigning. He defeated Taft in New Hampshire by a margin of 46,661 votes to 35,888.

A heated race between the general and the senator was now taking shape. On April 12, 1952, Eisenhower asked to be relieved of his job at NATO so he could come home to fight for the Republican presidential nomination.

In the primary elections following New Hampshire's, Eisenhower carried New Jersey, Pennsylvania, Massachusetts, and Oregon. Taft won in Nebraska, Wisconsin, Illinois, West Virginia, and his home state of Ohio. Totaling all of the states that had primary elections, Taft had 2,794,736 votes to Eisenhower's 2,114,588. In the states that chose their convention delegates by state conventions rather than primary elec-

"Anybody is a damn fool if he actually seeks to be president."

tions, those who were solidly conservative supported Taft, and those who sided with the liberal wing of the party generally favored Eisenhower.

There were two other major candidates for the nomination, Harold Stassen of Minnesota and Governor Earl Warren of California. Stassen and Warren won the primaries in their own states, but neither had much support elsewhere.

A few weeks before the national convention, the Associated Press reported that Taft had a lead of 458 delegates to Eisenhower's 402, with 604 needed to nominate. But Taft's problem was that he had few states where he could find additional votes, while Ike was the second choice of almost all the delegates pledged to Warren and Stassen.

The Republican convention was held in early July in Chicago. The first major issue was whether to seat some of the Southern delegates whose credentials were questioned because they obviously favored Taft and had been endorsed by the national committee controlled by Taft supporters. To make sure that the Eisenhower forces won this battle, Senator Henry Cabot Lodge Jr. of Massachusetts proposed a "fair play amendment denying the pro-Taft delegations seated by the Taft-controlled national committee the right to vote on the challenge to their credentials."[2] This "fair play" proposal was approved by a margin of 110 votes, allowing Eisenhower delegates to be seated in place of the Taft delegates.

This opened the floodgates to a sweeping movement toward Eisenhower. On the first ballot, Eisenhower received 595 votes—just nine short of the nomination—to Taft's 500. Before the tally became official, many delegates switched their votes to climb on Ike's bandwagon. The final count was 845 votes for Eisenhower, 280 for Taft, and 77 for Warren.

Before a wildly enthusiastic convention with many delegates hoisting "I like Ike" banners or wearing buttons with the same inscription, the wartime hero stood beaming alongside his wife, Mamie. In his acceptance speech, he expressed his desire to lead "a crusade against a party too long in power."[3]

Eisenhower's choice as a running mate was Senator Richard M. Nixon of California, the thirty-nine-year-old leader in the fight against Communists ever since the Alger Hiss affair. He was nominated by acclamation with no opposition.

THE DEMOCRATS NOMINATE THEIR STANDARD BEARER

On March 2, President Truman had announced that he would not be a candidate for reelection, even though Congress had exempted him from the Twenty-second Amendment's prohibition of third terms. Securing the Democratic 1952 presidential nomination now was a wide-open race among several prominent politicians. These included Senator Estes Kefauver of Tennessee, Senator Richard Russell of Georgia, W. Averell Harriman, a New Yorker who was director of foreign aid under Truman, Senator Robert Kerr of Oklahoma, and Vice President Alben W. Barkley, who was well liked by Democrats but stood little chance of winning the nomination because he was seventy-four years old.

Another possible candidate was Adlai E. Stevenson, governor of Illinois. But Stevenson was reluctant to plunge into the race. "I just don't want to run for the presidency," he firmly declared. "I have no desire for the office, mentally, temperamentally, or physically."[4]

Asked what he would do if nominated, he wryly replied, "I'll shoot myself." His only political desire was to be reelected governor of Illinois. Taking a slap at Eisenhower's popularity, Stevenson declared that personalities are irrelevant and candidates should be judged solely by their ability to address issues "sensibly and truthfully."[5]

Senator Kefauver had become a national figure by heading a Senate committee's televised investigation of organized crime. The lanky Tennessean, often wearing his familiar coonskin cap, campaigned successfully in several state primaries and attracted many young voters, moral reformers, and both urban and rural Democrats who liked his simply spoken message and folksy ways.

Kefauver, however, had many enemies in the Democratic Party. He was accused of promoting only himself and not being a good team player. Also, his crime investigation had incurred the wrath of some politicians, whom he charged with having ties to gangsters and gamblers. And the early announcement of his presidential candidacy without consulting Democratic Party leaders—at a time when President Truman was still expected to run—did not sit well with the party chieftains.

The Democrats opened their 1952 convention in Chicago in late July. On the first ballot, Kefauver led with 340 votes to Stevenson's 273, Russell's 268, and Harriman's 123½.

The second ballot showed the three front-runners all gaining more votes. Then, during a recess, Harriman and Massachusetts's favorite son, Governor Paul Dever, both withdrew and asked their supporters to vote for Stevenson.

The Illinois governor won a narrow majority on the third ballot, garnering 617½ votes from the 1,230 delegates. The selection of Stevenson marked the first time that a reluctant presidential candidate had succeeded since the nomination of James. A. Garfield by the Republicans in 1880.

Stevenson appeared before the convention and was introduced by President Truman. He "delivered a moving acceptance speech whose exalted, idealistic tone and expressive phraseology made it a classic of convention oratory."[6] Stevenson promised he would wage a vigorous campaign but warned, "Better we lose the election than mislead the people, and better we lose than misgovern the people."[7]

The delegates unanimously nominated Stevenson's choice for vice president, Senator John Sparkman of Alabama. Although he had opposed most civil rights legislation, Sparkman had compiled an otherwise liberal record during his sixteen years in the House of Representatives and the Senate.

To counter the Republicans' emphasis on ending the Korean War, corruption, and communism, the Democratic platform also included some strong points. It promised to introduce policies aimed at helping the working class, including improving Social Security by letting the elderly collect benefits while still holding a job. In education, the Democrats asked for federal financial assistance to state and local units; in contrast, the Republicans believed education was entirely the responsibility of local and state governments.

In foreign affairs, the Democrats' chief goal was stated as "peace with honor," which could be accomplished by strengthening the UN and promoting collective security by giving American assistance to allies around the world. The peaceful development of atomic energy was pledged, as was the use of atomic weapons, if needed, for national defense.

The civil rights plank of the party platform called for federal legislation to guarantee equal rights for minorities in voting, employment opportunities, and the achievement of personal safety.

Democratic presidential candidate Adlai Stevenson speaks at a campaign gathering in a small town in Ohio in 1952.

THE RACE FOR THE WHITE HOUSE

When Harry Truman ran for a second term in 1948, he campaigned throughout the country and traveled 31,000 miles (49,890 km), which set a new record for an incumbent. Truman traveled almost entirely by train, but by 1952 the vast improvements in airline service made more extensive itineraries possible. Eisenhower traveled 33,000 miles (53,108 km), mainly by airplanes, and made 228 speeches. Nixon, who was the Republicans' attack dog, logged 42,000 miles (67,592 km) and gave 375 speeches. Stevenson traveled 32,500 miles (52,303 km) and delivered 203 speeches.

Television played an important role in the 1952 election. Many of the candidates' major addresses were carried on television, and also, for the first time, there was a barrage of short political advertisements aimed at TV viewers. One example showed a black man saying to Eisenhower, "General, the Democrats are telling me I've never had it so good." Eisenhower replies, "Can that be true when America is billions in debt, when prices have doubled, when taxes break our backs, and we are still fighting in Korea? It's tragic and it's time for a change."[8]

Democrats felt offended by the steady stream of Republican TV ads. A Stevenson spokesman deplored the "high powered hucksters of Madison Avenue" and claimed that Republican ad agencies were trying to merchandise an inferior political ticket "in precisely the way they sell soap, ammoniated tooth paste, hair tonic or bubble gum." Stevenson himself declared, "This isn't Ivory Soap versus Palmolive."[9]

Just as the Republican machine seemed to be moving triumphantly, it suddenly became temporarily derailed. On September 18, there was a large headline in the *New York Post:* "SECRET NIXON FUND." The article disclosed that sixty-six wealthy Californians had set up a slush fund of more than $18,000 for Nixon when he was in the Senate. "The news hit the front pages of newspapers throughout the country and Republicans panicked while Democrats chortled."[10]

Some Republican leaders thought Nixon should withdraw immediately from the ticket, and they wondered how they could wage a campaign against corruption if their own vice presidential nominee was possibly corrupt. Eisenhower was angered by the revelation and urged Nixon to appear on television to defend himself. Ike bluntly said that the only way Nixon could stay on the ticket was to prove that he was "as clean as a hound's tooth."[11]

On September 23, Nixon spoke to the nation, fighting to keep alive his political career. Fifty-eight million people watched him, the largest audience in the history of television until the first 1960 debate between Nixon and John F. Kennedy.

In a highly dramatic, sometimes tearful manner, Nixon explained that the so-called slush fund was used entirely for legitimate political purposes, not for his personal living expenses. He said that he earned only a modest salary as a senator—not enough to pay for all of his political needs. He told the TV audience that his family had to cut corners to pay the mortgage on their home. They drove an old car, and his wife Pat had no mink coat but just a respectable Republican cloth coat.

"We did get something, a gift, after the nomination," he continued. "It was a little cocker spaniel dog . . . and our little girl Tricia, the six-year-old, named it Checkers. And you know, the kids, like all kids, loved the dog, and I just want to say this, right now, that regardless what they say about it, we are going to keep it."[12] Afterward, this address was always called the "Checkers speech."

Nixon closed his speech by appealing to the television viewers to contact the Republican National Committee and tell whether they felt he should stay on the ticket. An avalanche of telegrams and letters poured into the Republican headquarters praising Nixon. When the young senator flew to meet Eisenhower and hear his decision, the beaming general embraced him and warmly proclaimed, "You're my boy!"[13]

Eisenhower, in a speech on October 24, promised that if he was elected he would personally go to Korea to help end the war honorably. This announcement was greeted with an overwhelmingly favorable response from the American public. Polls that previously had shown Ike with a slight lead over Stevenson now revealed that he was the certain winner.

On Election Day, Eisenhower won a stunning victory. He received 33,936,234 votes—more than any other presidential candidate in history—to Stevenson's 27,314,992 votes. Ike carried 39 states with 442 electoral votes, while Stevenson won only 9 states, all in the South, with 89 electoral votes.

When Eisenhower was inaugurated in 1953, the United States was much different than it is today. The population was

On September 23, Nixon spoke to the nation, fighting to keep alive his political career.

about 160 million compared to more than 281 million in 2002. The median family income in 1953 was $4,242, and it was $48,950 at the dawn of the twenty-first century. Another astounding change was that only 56 percent of American households had TV sets when Ike became president, compared to 98 percent in 2002.

THE REMATCH IN 1956

President Eisenhower suffered a heart attack in September 1955. Sixty-five-year-old Ike was the oldest president in the twentieth century until Ronald Reagan was elected in 1980 at age sixty-nine. Considering his health and age, many people believed that Eisenhower would not run for a second term. But Ike was desperately needed by the Republican Party. Nixon probably would have been the presidential candidate if Eisenhower stepped aside, but a poll taken in January 1956 showed Stevenson leading Nixon by 55 percent to 38 percent.

Eisenhower recovered from his heart attack, and in March 1956 announced that he would seek a second term. He said that he would require "a regime of ordered work activity, interspersed with regular amounts of exercise, recreation and rest."[14] Then in June he had surgery for an intestinal disorder called ileitus, but again he recovered and looked forward to the upcoming campaign.

The Republican convention was held in late August in San Francisco. The delegates voted unanimously for the ticket of Eisenhower and Nixon.

The Democrats held their convention in Chicago a week before the Republican convention. Stevenson easily won the nomination, although former president Truman supported Governor W. Averell Harriman of New York and criticized Stevenson as a defeatist.

In an unusual move, Stevenson declared that he would not personally select his running mate and would leave this decision to the convention. Thirteen names were placed in nomi-

Preparing to run for his second term in office in 1956, President Dwight Eisenhower laughs as his wife, Mamie, tries on a cardboard eye shade that says "I Like Ike."

nation for vice president. On the first ballot, the three leaders were Senators Estes Kefauver of Tennessee, John F. Kennedy of Massachusetts, and Albert Gore of Tennessee, the father of the Democrats' presidential candidate in 2000.

Kennedy moved into the lead on the second ballot and was fewer than 40 votes short of the nomination. Then Gore announced that he was withdrawing in favor of his Tennessee colleague, and this started a bandwagon for Kefauver as other states followed Gore's lead. The final tally showed Kefauver with 755½ votes to Kennedy's 589. (Had Kennedy won the vice presidential nomination in 1956 and gone down to defeat with Stevenson, many political experts believe that he would not have been the Democrats' presidential candidate in 1960.)

Eisenhower did less campaigning in 1956 than in 1952, partly because of his health and partly because he felt confident that he would win. Nixon campaigned much more actively, traveling 42,000 miles (67,592 km), but he dropped the anti-Communist theme that had been expressed in all of his previous political races because in 1956 it was no longer such a popular issue. After the chaotic McCarthy hearings, Nixon did not want to be labeled another irate warmonger.

Stevenson spoke in favor of helping senior citizens, addressing the plight of poor people, expanding health care, and securing better education for all Americans. Most of these goals were later achieved in John Kennedy's New Frontier and Lyndon Johnson's Great Society.

When Americans voted on November 6, Eisenhower did even better than he had done in 1952. Receiving 35,590,472 votes to Stevenson's 26,022,752 votes, the popular president carried 41 of the 48 states with 457 electoral votes. Stevenson won only 7 states with 73 electoral votes. Ike carried 6 of the southern states in this once solidly Democratic region, beginning the trend that later resulted in most Southern states voting for the Republican presidential candidate.

The 1956 election was really another personal victory for the greatly admired man in the White House. The nation appreciated Eisenhower's many accomplishments in his first term. He outran the Republican candidates for congressional seats by more than 6 million votes, and the Democrats won the Senate, 49 to 47, and the House of Representatives, 234 to 201.

FOUR

African Americans Seek Racial Justice

At the beginning of the 1950s, there were many signs of discrimination against African Americans. In many parts of the United States, blacks were barred from hotels and restaurants that served white patrons. Segregation was especially prevalent throughout the South. There blacks were forced to live as second-class citizens.

They had to attend separate churches and segregated schools that were usually much inferior to the schools for white students. African Americans had to sit in specified sections of buses, trains, theaters, and even ballparks. They had to use separate restrooms and water fountains.

Blacks were compelled to live in certain parts of southern towns and cities, where the housing was generally inadequate and diseases were rampant. Black patients usually were treated only by black doctors, and they were denied admittance to most clinics and hospitals.

Lynchings and other physical abuses of blacks continued in the South. Destructive raids by the Ku Klux Klan and other white supremacist groups struck terror in the hearts of many African Americans. Denied the right to vote throughout nearly all of the South, blacks appeared to have little chance to escape their miserable conditions.

In 1892, Homer Plessy, a man who was one-eighth black (one of his eight great-grandparents was black) and who could easily have passed for white, had boarded a railroad in New Orleans and sat in the whites-only coach. The conductor requested that he move to the car for blacks in the back of the train. When Plessy refused, a train detective arrested him. Plessy filed a lawsuit that reached the U.S. Supreme Court in 1896.

The lawyer for Plessy argued that a state may not label one citizen as white and another as black in the common pursuit of daily activities. He insisted that the Thirteenth Amendment banned not only slavery but also "a caste, a legal condition of subjection to the dominant class."[1]

The Supreme Court did not accept his argument. In *Plessy v. Ferguson*, by a vote of eight to one, it ruled that under the equal protection clause of the Fourteenth Amendment, a state could provide "separate but equal" facilities for African Americans. Justice Henry B. Brown, speaking for the majority, said that people will never deviate from their own customs and traditions and that those who drafted the Fourteenth Amendment "could not have intended to abolish distinctions based on color." It was not the law that "stamps the colored race with the badge of inferiority," Brown concluded, "but their own feelings about it."[2]

Justice John Marshall Harlan, the lone dissenter in this famous case, argued that "in view of the Constitution, in the eye of the law, there is in this country no superior, dominant ruling class of citizens. . . . Our Constitution is color-blind, and neither knows nor tolerates classes among citizens. In respect of civil rights, all citizens are equal before the law."[3]

Although *Plessy* v. *Ferguson* literally pertained only to separation of blacks and whites on trains, its "separate but equal" clause soon was applied to all forms of segregation in the South. These separate facilities were almost never equal because white southerners regarded blacks as inferior. More than half a century passed before this situation was changed.

A 1954 COURT DECISION AGAINST SEGREGATION

Five legal attacks on school segregation reached the Supreme Court in 1952, with cases filed in Kansas, Virginia, South Carolina, Delaware, and the District of Columbia. The justices consolidated all five under a single name, *Brown* v. *Board of Education of Topeka, Kansas*.

A welder named Oliver Brown had sued in Kansas on behalf of his daughter Linda. She had been forced to travel a long distance to a rundown school for blacks. Linda had to walk six blocks through a dangerous railway switching yard and then take a bus for another twenty-one blocks. A whites-only school with better facilities and more experienced teachers was only seven blocks from her home. Oliver Brown believed that his daughter should be permitted to attend this much closer school that offered better educational opportunities.

Nearly two years passed before the Supreme Court took up this controversial case. Chief Justice Fred Vinson, who probably would have supported continued segregation, stalled the proceedings. "Congress did not pass a statute deterring or ordering no segregation," Vinson stated. "We can't close our eyes to the seriousness of the problem. We face the complete abolition of the public school system."[4]

Vinson died suddenly of a heart attack in September 1953. President Eisenhower filled this vacancy on the Court by appointing Earl Warren the new chief justice. Warren was the

Thurgood Marshall poses outside of the Supreme Court building in 1958, where he had argued Brown v. Board of Education four years earlier. In 1967, President Lyndon Johnson appointed him to the Supreme Court. Marshall was the first African American to serve on the Court.

liberal Republican governor of California. Eisenhower may have made this appointment because Warren had helped him win the presidency in 1952 by withdrawing his own candidacy and asking his delegates to vote for Ike.

Although he had previously been attorney general of California, Warren had never served as a judge. But he had some strong beliefs that he intended to implement on the Supreme Court. They were equality for every American, improved education, and the right of young people to have a decent life.

The National Association for the Advancement of Colored People (NAACP) hired Thurgood Marshall, an outstanding black attorney who had previously won thirteen of fifteen cases before the Supreme Court, to represent Brown in this historic case. Marshall argued that segregation made equal education impossible and that separate schools damaged black youngsters, making them feel inferior. (In 1967, President Lyndon Johnson appointed Marshall to the Supreme Court, thus making him the first African American ever to sit on that bench.)

Chief Justice Warren was convinced that Marshall's reasoning was correct. Then he worked hard to convince the other justices, including the three southerners, to follow his lead. He knew that in such a controversial case it was important to have a large majority of justices agree with the decision.

On May 17, 1954, the Supreme Court voted unanimously to uphold the claim made on behalf of black students. "To separate [them] from others of similar age and qualifications solely because of their race," declared Chief Justice Warren, "generates a feeling of inequality as to their status in the community that may affect their hearts and minds in a way never to be undone. . . . We conclude that in the field of public education the doctrine of 'separate but equal' has no place. Separate educational facilities are inherently unequal."[5]

The Supreme Court did not say how the states should change their school systems to eliminate segregation. It was not until the next year that the Court announced a vague standard that the states should accomplish integration with "all deliberate speed," but, concerned about civil disorder, it set no rigid schedule for compliance.

Gradually, some states worked toward reducing segregation. After many months, Texas, West Virginia, Tennessee, Maryland, Arkansas, and Delaware reported partial integration in 350 schools.

In the Deep South, however, reaction to *Brown* v. *Board of Education* was extremely hostile. Some states, including South Carolina and Georgia, even threatened to close their public schools rather than integrate them. Governor Herman Talmadge of Georgia claimed the Supreme Court "has blatantly ignored all law and precedent" and pledged that his state would "map a program to insure continued and permanent segregation of the races."[6]

In the wake of the Court ruling, there was a rash of violent actions in various places. In 1955, Emmett Till, a black fourteen year old from Chicago, was visiting relatives in Greenwood, Mississippi. When it was alleged that he had insulted a white woman, white men dragged him from his relatives' house, and one of them shot the boy in the head. They then wired his body to a heavy piece of metal and threw it in a river. Witnesses identified the murderers to federal agents, but an all-white jury acquitted the men.

The following year belligerent whites in Clinton, Tennessee, forcibly prevented twelve African-American students from enrolling in the local high school. At about the same time, in Mansfield, Texas, four hundred angry white men barged into a high school where a federal court had ordered the integration of three blacks, and they caused such an uproar that the frightened students quickly withdrew.

THE CRISIS AT LITTLE ROCK

No one thought that the biggest battle for school integration would erupt in Little Rock, Arkansas. Shortly after the *Brown* v. *Board of Education* decision, the Little Rock school board had approved a plan for gradual desegregation starting at the high school level. Arkansas's medical and law schools already had been integrated. Only nine African-American students were scheduled to join the two thousand white ones when Central High School opened its fall semester on September 3, 1957.

Even though a U.S. district court had ordered that school segregation must end soon in Little Rock, Governor Orval Faubus decided to call out the Arkansas National Guard to block integration. On the Sunday before school was to open, Winthrop Rockefeller, a member of the famous Rockefeller family, who lived in Arkansas, rushed to the statehouse and tried to persuade Faubus not to use the National Guard at Central High School.

"I'm sorry but I'm already committed," the governor said. "I'm going to run for a third term, and if I don't do this, Jim Johnson and Bruce Bennett [two segregationists who were running against him] will tear me to shreds."[7] Governor Faubus's intent was to put his own political future above the welfare of black students in his state.

By the time the first class bell sounded at Central High School, an angry mob of nearly a thousand men had gathered in front of the campus. Someone cried out that the Negroes had arrived. But these blacks were not students; they were four African-American reporters who had arrived together. Retreating, they were chased by a group of bullies who caught and beat them. The nine African-American students were frightened and fled.

With the state National Guard patrolling the area and the mob growing larger and even more hostile, President Eisenhower stated, "The federal law and orders of a United States District Court . . . cannot be flouted with immunity by

Black students are escorted by soldiers of the 101st Airborne Division on their first day of school at Central High in Little Rock, Arkansas. The soldiers were sent by President Eisenhower to protect the students and ensure that desegregation, now federal law, was carried out.

any individual or any mob of extremists. I will use the full power of the United States including whatever force may be necessary to prevent any obstruction of the law and to carry out the orders of the Federal Court."[8]

Eisenhower met with Faubus and tried to get him to back down. But the stubborn governor declared after their meeting that he would continue to use the National Guard to prevent black students from enrolling at Central High School.

On September 24, President Eisenhower took action, even though he wasn't convinced that force should be used to achieve desegregation. He sent in troops of the 101st Airborne Division and put the Arkansas National Guard under federal control to protect the nine black students when they entered the high school. These soldiers guarded the students for many months, until tempers eased and quiet was restored.

The crisis at Little Rock was the first time since the period following the Civil War that federal troops were sent into the South to preserve order. It seemed that *Brown* v. *Board of Education*, which had held the promise of equality for students, was only a partial victory in the long struggle of blacks to achieve their civil rights.

A SEAMSTRESS CAUSES A MAJOR BUS BOYCOTT

Rosa Parks had endured the unfairness of the bus service in Montgomery, Alabama, all of her life. Blacks had to sit in the back of the bus, and when the white sections were filled, they had to stand so white people could use their seats.

On December 1, 1955, Parks had worked all day as a seamstress and then shopped for groceries. She was going home on a crowded bus, and when a white man boarded, she was ordered by the driver to give up her seat. Refusing to do so, she was arrested and jailed. "The time had just come when I had been pushed as far as I could stand to be pushed," she later said. "I had decided that I would have to know once and for all what rights I had as a human being and a citizen."[9]

"The time

had just

come when I

had been

pushed as far

as I could

stand to be

pushed."

Parks knew what she was doing in challenging Alabama's segregation law. She was secretary of the Montgomery chapter of the NAACP, and its head, Reverend E. D. Nixon, had been seeking an incident that would provide a court fight over bus segregation in his city. Nixon bailed Parks out of jail and asked her to be the central figure in a case before a federal court.

She agreed to do so "if it will mean something to Montgomery." Her mother and husband were appalled by her courageous decision. "The white folks will kill you," said her distraught husband.[10]

Nixon decided that the following Monday all blacks should boycott Montgomery's bus system. He enlisted about fifty black ministers, who passed the message to their congregations at Sunday church services. Among them was the new twenty-six-year-old preacher at the Dexter Avenue Baptist Church, Martin Luther King Jr., who soon became president of a new group called the Montgomery Improvement Association.

On Monday morning the buses had no black passengers, even though customarily blacks made up the largest group of bus riders. Later that day, King addressed the bus boycott at his church. Every seat was taken, and many in the crowd—estimated at between 10,000 and 15,000—had to listen from speakers installed outside the building.

"There comes a time when people get tired of being trampled over by the iron feet of oppression," King declared. "Now let us say we are not advocating violence. . . . The only weapon we have in our hands is the weapon of protest. But the great glory of American democracy is the right to protest for right." He closed his powerful speech by imploring, "If we are wrong—justice is a lie."[11]

This was the beginning of King's outstanding career as the foremost black leader in the long struggle to achieve civil rights for his people, a career that ultimately was rewarded by his becoming the only person besides a president for whom a national holiday was established. Probably the key to King's enormous success was his absolute insistence that the movement he championed must be carried forward in a nonviolent, peaceful manner. Taking his tactics from the passive resistance of India's Mohandas Gandhi, King always told his followers that they should meet hate with love.

The black community in Montgomery responded whole-heartedly to the bus boycott. More than three hundred volunteer drivers moved the boycotters between their homes and work sites. Other blacks traveled long distances on foot or by bicycle. The white mayor predicted that "comes the first rainy day and the Negroes will be back on the buses."[12] The rain soon came, but the boycott continued.

White Montgomery leaders tried to strike back. Their nearly empty buses were causing huge financial losses. They stopped black cabdrivers from carrying people to and from work in groups of five or six for ten cents a ride because a city ordinance said that the minimum fare for a ride had to be forty-five cents. The police began arresting blacks for slight violations of the law. King himself was arrested for driving 30 miles (48 km) an hour in a 25-mile (40-km)-per-hour zone. Two days later, his house was bombed.

Later, King and other black leaders were arrested because the huge car pool allegedly was a business enterprise operating without a license. They were tried in a state court. If the car pool was declared illegal, the bus boycott would have had to end.

In the midst of the trial, electrifying news arrived. On November 13, 1956, the U.S. Supreme Court declared that all laws requiring bus segregation were unconstitutional.

When the boycott ended, King boarded a bus and sat in a front seat. Afterward, he said that it was a great ride.

(50 America in the 1950s)

FIVE

The Cold War Escalates

some scientists who had worked on the atom bomb opposed any effort to build an even more deadly bomb. Albert Einstein, the brilliant mathematician, was very worried about what could happen if more atom bombs were dropped anyplace in the world. In 1950, he observed that "radioactive poisoning of the atmosphere and hence annihilation of any life on earth has been brought within the range of technical possibilities."[1]

Still, there were important reasons for developing a superbomb much more powerful than the atom bomb. Americans were concerned that the Soviet Union was eager to expand its control over vast areas. There also was concern because the Soviets had a much larger army than those of the United States and its allies. But the most important reason was the awful possibility that the Soviet Union would build the superbomb first.

"I don't think you have a choice," Rear Admiral Sidney Souers of the National Security Council told President Truman. "It's either we make it or wait until the Russians drop one on us without warning."[2]

On January 31, 1950, President Truman decided that work on the hydrogen bomb would begin.

A TORRENT OF DEVASTATING WEAPONS

The atom bomb was based on nuclear fission, while the hydrogen bomb was based on fusing together atoms of hydrogen, the same element that fuels the sun. The heat at the center of this superbomb was at least five times as great as that at the interior of the sun, and it had the force of five million tons of TNT.

On November 1, 1952, the first test of the H-bomb took place at Eniwetok, a mile-wide atoll in the Pacific Ocean's Marshall Islands. Its fury surprised even the scientists who observed it through special glasses on planes and ships 50 miles (80 km) away. Its nuclear matter rose like a gigantic cloud about 25 miles (40 km) into the stratosphere and spread 100 miles (161 km) across the sky. The H-bomb gouged out such a huge crater that all of Eniwetok disappeared.

If this device had exploded in the United States, it was estimated that it would have obliterated entire cities. Scientists believed that if the H-bomb were dropped on New York City, for example, its fireball would cause such a giant crater that the Hudson and East rivers would be joined and together they would divide Manhattan into two separate islands.

People throughout the world were terrified because now there was a weapon capable of destroying all of civilization. In addition to decimating cities, its radioactive element had the power to end all forms of life. Americans prayed that the Soviet

The Red Scare affected every-day citizens, too. Americans felt threatened that they could become the victims of deadly bomb attacks. In the public schools during the fifties, students participated in drills designed to protect them from falling bombs. At the signal "drop," they jumped from their seats and scurried

Above: Students at a school in Brooklyn, New York, practice a "duck and cover" drill.
Left: A California mother and her children make a practice run for their backyard bomb shelter.

beneath desks and tables, where they shielded their heads under their arms. Or they filed from their classrooms into school halls and stood with their backs against strong walls.

Some families were so frightened about the specter of bombs destroying their houses that they had companies build in their backyards expensive concrete shelters with steel tops and stairs to the bottom. They usually equipped the shelters with a radio, supplies of water and canned foods, and games and toys for the children. Anxious neighbors often asked the shelter owners if they had room for their families, too.

Union would not be able to develop the same weapon. But their fears came true when there was a Soviet H-bomb explosion in Siberia in 1953, just nine months after the U.S. test.

The U.S. Strategic Air Command had planes that carried the new superbombs, and they patrolled the skies day and night. The navy constructed carriers large enough to carry nuclear bombs, and in 1954 it launched the *Nautilus*, the first atomic-powered submarine. It had the ability to shoot nuclear weapons while submerged.

Scientists in the Soviet Union concentrated on developing missiles that could be sent long distances with nuclear devices. In 1957, it tested the world's first intercontinental ballistic missile (ICBM). A short time later, the United States also developed the ICBM, and by the end of the 1950s, the American missile program had surged ahead of the Soviets'.

EISENHOWER TRIES TO EASE TENSIONS

President Eisenhower was deeply concerned about the deadly Cold War scenario in which the two superpowers were doomed to eye each other indefinitely across a trembling world.

He delivered an "Atoms for Peace" speech to the UN in December 1953. In this address, he proposed an international agency that would stockpile uranium and nuclear materials in order "to serve the needs rather than the fears of mankind." He promised that the "United States would devote its entire heart and mind to find the way by which the miraculous inventiveness of man shall not be dedicated to his death, but consecrated to his life."[3]

His proposal led to the creation of the International Atomic Energy Agency. But this organization did not stop the arms race because the Soviets perceived it as nothing more than American propaganda.

A year and a half later, President Eisenhower attended a summit meeting at Geneva, Switzerland. There he talked with

Nikita Khrushchev, the head of the Soviet Union, and the government leaders of Great Britain and France.

Eisenhower boldly called for an open skies policy by which the four countries would give each other a blueprint of their military establishments and permit aerial inspections of these military bases. "Khrushchev, suspicious of American intentions, perhaps fearful that the United States would learn too much about relative Soviet weakness if granted broad access to Soviet airspace, was not interested."[4]

The president's peace efforts were countered somewhat by tough-minded Secretary of State John Foster Dulles. In January 1954, Dulles announced a policy that became known as massive retaliation. He argued the need "to depend primarily upon a great capacity to retaliate, instantly, by means and at places of our own choosing," which implied "nuclear attacks against Soviet cities."[5]

Dulles believed that the United States must be willing to go to the brink of war if necessary to protect American interests. His critics called this "brinksmanship" and feared that it was a dangerous policy in a decade when warfare could lead to nuclear annihilation.

CRISES IN DIFFERENT PLACES

After Japan surrendered Indochina in 1945, the French attempted to resume their pre–World War II occupation of that former colony. But the natives who lived in Indochina were tired of French imperialism and eager to achieve independence. Their strongest leader, Ho Chi Minh, was a dedicated Communist, trained in the Soviet Union and China. He headed a group called the Vietminh that started a war in 1946 to drive the French out of Indochina.

The United States was unwilling to abandon Indochina to the Communists. President Eisenhower admitted that this region was of only slight importance to the United States. But he believed "what came to be known as the 'domino theory': if Indochina fell [to Communists], the remaining states of Southeast Asia would fall one after another."[6] To help prevent this from happening, the United States was sending about $1 billion a year in aid to the French cause in Indochina.

Despite this financial help, in 1954 the French army in the key fortress of Dien Bien Phu was besieged by the Communists. Since a military disaster threatened, the question arose: Should the United States enter the war?

Vice President Nixon and Secretary of State Dulles favored intervention with American bombings to help bail out the beleaguered French. Eisenhower, however, insisted on congressional approval and a British agreement to join forces with the United States before Americans would enter the war. Neither of these requirements occurred.

After Dien Bien Phu fell, a multination conference divided the area of Indochina known as Vietnam into two parts, Communist North Vietnam and anti-Communist South Vietnam. This temporary partition was to be followed by an all-Vietnam election in 1956, but this did not take place. Ho Chi Minh was confident that he would win this election and did not care that it was delayed, because he intended to bring about by military force a united Communist Vietnam.

The United States sent financial aid and military advisers to South Vietnam, which was controlled by Ngo Dinh Diem, a greedy and corrupt politician. American military forces did not become actively involved in the Vietnam War until 1964, when Lyndon B. Johnson was president.

Events elsewhere were moving fast. In 1956, the people of Hungary mounted the most serious challenge to Soviet rule in Eastern Europe. On November 1, Hungarian leader Imry Nagy protested Soviet troop movements in his country, repudiated the Warsaw Pact that bound the Soviet puppet states together in a military alliance, and declared Hungary's neutrality. He also cabled the secretary-general of the UN, requesting that Hungarian neutrality be put on the agenda of the UN General Assembly.

Deng Xiaoping, a leader of the Communist Chinese government, was visiting Moscow at this time. He told Khrushchev that the Hungarian rebels were anti-Communist and must be put down. On November 3, fifteen Soviet army divisions and four thousand tanks were sent to Budapest, Hungary's capital.

Nagy broadcast on Radio Budapest that morning and said to the Hungarian people, "Today at daybreak, Soviet troops attacked our capital with the obvious intent of overthrowing the lawful democratic Hungarian government."[7] He promised not to surrender.

Many Hungarians believed that the United States would come to their aid. They had been listening for years to Radio Free Europe, a U.S.-backed station that broadcast into Eastern Europe, urging Hungary's "freedom fighters" to revolt.

President Eisenhower issued a strong protest against the Russian invasion of Hungary. But he and his advisers decided that it was much too dangerous to send military forces behind the Iron Curtain and try to rescue one of the nations controlled by the Soviet Union. They concluded that this would almost certainly trigger a nuclear war.

The UN tried to help by demanding that Soviet troops and tanks withdraw from Hungary. However, Khrushchev refused even to allow UN observers to come into Budapest.

While the Western world looked on in horror, the Hungarians were ruthlessly overpowered by the Soviets. Budapest became a slaughterhouse, and thousands of people fled in panic for the Austrian border because Austria was not controlled by the Soviets. The United States eventually changed its immigration laws to admit 30,000 Hungarian refugees.

At about the time of the Hungarian revolt, there was serious trouble in the Middle East. Egypt's president, Gamal Abdel Nasser, planned to build a large dam at Aswan on the Nile River. Construction of this giant project would provide much electric power for Egypt's industries and farmlands. The United States and Great Britain offered to help finance the building of the dam, with an estimated cost of $1.3 billion.

SPUTNIK BEGINS
THE SPACE AGE

By today's standards it doesn't look like much, but when <u>sputnik</u> was launched by
the Soviets on October 4, 1957, it caused a sensation. The size of a large beach ball,
and with four legs extending outward, it was displayed at the 1958 World's Fair in
Brussels, Belgium.

ANOTHER TYPE OF RIVALRY between the Soviet Union and the United States captured headlines in the late 1950s. On October 4, 1957, *Sputnik* (which means "fellow traveler") was launched in Russia. The first satellite to investigate outer space, it was an aluminum sphere about 22 inches (56 centimeters) in diameter and weighing 184 pounds (83 kilograms). *Sputnik* carried a radio transmitter, and when it entered orbit it sent radio bleeps that were heard around the world.

Americans were shocked and humiliated by this enormous Soviet accomplishment. Scientist Edward Teller, who had been credited with developing the hydrogen bomb, said on television that the United States had lost "a battle more important and greater than Pearl Harbor." James Killian, president of the Massachusetts Institute of Technology, later declared, "What I felt most keenly was the affront to my national pride."[8]

People in the United States were not only ashamed that the Russians had moved ahead of them in developing new technology. They also knew that Soviet missiles soon could carry nuclear warheads aimed at their soil.

Sputnik II, launched by the Soviets on November 3, carried a dog, Laika, the first living thing to travel in orbit. This proved that life could endure in the weightlessness of space and pointed to the day when men and women in satellites could orbit Earth.

Scientists and military strategists demanded that the United States catch up with the Russians in this important race. Fortunately, Americans already were developing rocketry. Two months after the launch of *Sputnik*, the U.S. rocket *Vanguard* lifted off, carrying a small 4-pound (2 kg) satellite intended for orbit. But it rose just 2 feet (.6 meter) off the ground, fell back to earth, and exploded. The spectators at Cape Canaveral, Florida, were deeply disappointed.

In January 1958, the United States finally entered the space race successfully. The rocket *Explorer* launched a satellite into orbit. Americans hailed *Explorer* with happiness and a deep feeling of relief. "That's wonderful," President Eisenhower declared. "I sure feel a lot better now."[9]

Soon additional American satellites were orbiting the Earth. The nation heard President Eisenhower's 1958 Christmas message relayed by satellite from outer space.

One of the lasting achievements of the space race was the passing by Congress of the National Defense Education Act of 1958. It provided a huge spending of federal dollars to improve the country's educational system, including loans to college students majoring in engineering, science, and mathematics.

Nasser delayed accepting this offer because he felt he might receive more money from the Soviet Union, which wanted to extend its influence among the Arab countries in the Middle East. His threat to bargain with the Soviets for better terms caused the United States and Britain to withdraw their offer to help pay for the Aswan Dam. Furious, Nasser seized and nationalized the Suez Canal on July 26, 1956. Previously the canal had been open to all vessels except those from Israel, the Arabs' chief enemy.

On October 29, Israel, which had recently fought back terrorist raids launched inside Egypt, attacked that country and moved its troops toward the canal. Two days later, Britain and France ordered their planes to bomb Egyptian bases, and on November 5, their paratroopers started seizing the northern parts of the canal.

The action was taken without consulting the United States, which was shocked by this secret offensive waged by three of its closest friends. Tension heightened when the Soviet government threatened to send "volunteer" troops to help Egypt and possibly start a nuclear war against Britain and France.

The UN General Assembly was quickly convened to deal with this frightening situation. The United States took the unusual step of voting with the Soviet Union to help pass a resolution condemning the military action taken by Britain, France, and Israel. The UN then ordered that the invading forces be pulled out of Egypt, and a special UN patrol was sent to preserve order while they retreated.

One writer later observed that this crisis "showed the impossibility of British and French Governments trying to play Great Powers against the will of America, Russia and most other nations."[10]

The Soviet Union's belligerent attitude toward the enemies of Egypt in the Suez Canal war appeared to open the door to possible Communist penetration of the oil-rich Middle East. To prevent this from happening, President Eisenhower in January 1957 received from Congress the power to use American military forces to defend the Middle East. Known as the Eisenhower Doctrine, this policy told the world that the Middle East would not be subject to Communist aggression.

The Eisenhower Doctrine was put into operation in July 1958 after the pro-Western monarch of Iraq, King Faisal II, was assassinated by army officers who were in league with both the Soviet Union and Egypt's Nasser. Their action threatened the two small nearby nations of Lebanon and Jordan, where subversives were plotting to overthrow the governments. At the request of the Lebanese president, the United States boldly landed about ten thousand troops in Lebanon, and two days later two thousand British paratroopers landed in Jordan.

The UN provided a solution to this problem. In return for guarantees that Lebanon and Jordan would be safe from subversion or invasion, the American and British forces were withdrawn. President Eisenhower's energetic action served notice that the United States was unwilling to travel the road to appeasement.

TROUBLE ON OUR DOORSTEP

On January 8, 1959, a guerrilla band led by Fidel Castro overturned the corrupt government of Cuba, which had impoverished the Cuban people, and a month later he became prime minister of that island country. Castro promised that he would bring sweeping changes to Cuba—to its government, its economy, and the way of life for its people.

His soldiers rounded up many of his enemies, who were charged with committing crimes against the revolution. Some were publicly executed; others were sentenced to long terms in prison. "Journalists and members of Congress in the United States condemned Castro's 'blood bath,' claiming that his brutal treatment of enemies was similar to the way Russia disposed of its dissenters."[11]

Many Cubans fled from their homeland when Castro came to power. About 500,000 Cuban exiles settled in or near Miami, Florida. Today, about half the population of Greater Miami is Cuban.

Castro ordered in May 1959 that many huge farms in his nation were to be broken up. Nearly 9 million acres (3,642,120 hectares) of land, some belonging to U.S. companies, were seized by the Cuban government. The following year, Castro demanded that the oil refineries on the island, which were owned by Americans, must refine oil that Cuba was receiving from the Soviet Union. When the oil companies refused to do this, Castro seized their refineries.

In 1960, the Eisenhower administration struck back. It put an embargo on all trade with Cuba. The island's economy, which had depended to a large extent on selling its huge sugar crop to the United States, was severely crippled by this embargo.

In the same year, however, Cuba made a major trade agreement with the Soviet Union in which the Soviet Union promised to buy 1 million tons of Cuban sugar annually for the next five years. The Soviets also pledged that Cuba would receive machinery, oil, wheat, and other Soviet products, plus a loan of $100 million for buying industrial equipment.

It became clear that Castro was a pro-Soviet Communist, which he formally proclaimed in 1961. At about the same time that President Eisenhower was leaving office in January 1961, relations between the United States and Cuba were officially broken off. But the presence of a Communist dictator in a place so near the United States caused trouble on our doorstep for many years to come.

Fidel Castro during a historic visit to the United Nations in 1960

SIX

Big Changes Come to the United States

Except for brief recessions in 1953 and 1957–1958, large numbers of Americans enjoyed prosperity in the 1950s. "Even the American taste for superlatives was stretched by the nature of the good times in the fifties," observed historian Harold Evans. "There had been nothing like it before in the history of the world."[1]

Personal incomes nearly tripled between 1940 and 1955, and the number of persons who held jobs rose from about 53 million in 1950 to more than 70 million by 1960. The United States, with 6 percent of the world's population, was consuming one-third of the world's goods and services.

Stock market prices soared to a new high, and basic industries such as automobiles, steel, and oil flourished. This was the decade that also produced some exciting new technologies. Computers came into much wider use, although they still were very large and unwieldy. For example, during the 1952 presidential election, the computers that tallied the votes occupied a space as large as the average family's living room.

There were also important developments in other electronics. For the first time, people had access to cordless transistor radios and high fidelity, which electronically reproduces sound without distortion.

Americans had improved lifestyles in the 1950s. Most families by then had vacuum cleaners and refrigerators. Vacuum cleaners made it much easier to remove dirt from carpets and rugs than using brooms and dustpans. Refrigerators replaced the old iceboxes, in which men had to deposit heavy blocks of ice regularly. The large assortment of recently developed frozen foods reduced the number of trips to the grocery store. Some homes and most theaters and auditoriums had air-conditioning, which made life more comfortable during hot summers.

People in the United States lived better and longer in the 1950s than ever before. They were generally about 3 inches (8 cm) taller than Americans at the beginning of the century. A woman in 1950 could expect to live to the age of seventy-one, twenty years longer than a woman in 1900. A man's life expectancy climbed from forty-eight to sixty-five. The overall population also was younger. Because of a "baby boom," which accounted for an astounding 40 million births from 1950 to 1960, about 40 percent of the American people were under twenty years of age by the mid-1960s.

THE CHANGING ROLES OF WOMEN

During World War II, when many men were serving in the armed forces, millions of American women, including those who were married, were employed in defense plants or held important positions in various industries. After the men returned home from the war, this situation changed dramatically and impacted the 1950s. With a prospering economy in which husbands alone generally could support their families, their wives left the workforce in huge numbers.

In general, married women in the fifties were expected to perform the job of stay-at-home wives and mothers. The family was to be the center of their lives, and if it wasn't, they were often criticized for deviating from the norm.

This situation raised a serious question: What if women had come to enjoy their independence and did not want to give up their jobs? A woman's intelligence, energy, and creativity were now funneled into the single sphere of family life. The professions, except for teaching and nursing, were virtually closed to married women, and most of the jobs available to them paid poorly. Was this fair to married women? Weren't they being treated as second-class citizens?

Women's rights made no significant gains in the 1950s. Also, the opportunity for larger numbers of women to be elected to offices in local, state, and national government did not occur until later decades.

MOVING TO THE SUBURBS

During the depression of the 1930s and World War II, there was very limited construction of new houses. But in the prosperous fifties, with the population soaring, this situation changed dramatically. People had more money to spend on new homes.

The federal government helped people achieve their goal of owning a new home. Through the Federal Housing Administration and the Veterans Administration, which serviced the needs of former military personnel, the government made it possible for millions of people to buy single-family houses with low down payments and inexpensive, long-term loans.

In 1950 alone, 1.4 million new housing units were constructed. A large number of these homes were built in new suburbs rather than in existing cities. Families wanted to live in places where there was less traffic and noise; cleaner air; reduced crime; more green lawns, trees, and flowerbeds; and better schools for their children.

"The 1960 census revealed that while central cities had grown about 25 percent in population since 1950, the suburbs had increased over 50 percent. . . . Several central cities, including Detroit, St. Louis, San Francisco, and Washington, actually lost population, something unprecedented in the history of American cities."[2]

To service the sprouting suburbs, shopping centers were quickly erected. They were filled with stores, offices, and gas stations. This enabled suburbanites to travel only short distances to purchase the products they needed and to visit the offices of doctors, dentists, and lawyers.

There were many builders of new suburban homes, but the most famous was William Levitt, whose picture appeared on the cover of *Time* magazine on July 3, 1950. When Levitt opened his first sales office for homes he had built in a suburb of New York City, in Nassau County, on March 7, 1949, more than a thousand customers were waiting. "When the doors opened it was like the Oklahoma Land Rush of 1889, with the Young Marrieds, as they were now beginning to be called, rushing around, resolved to be among the first to buy the basic four-room houses for $6,900."[3]

Levittown, as the development was known, was very successful. Eventually it had thousands of homes that were occupied by more than 82,000 people.

William Levitt admitted that he had borrowed Henry Ford's production system used at the large Ford plant in Detroit, Michigan. But instead of producing cars on an assembly line, he had a different kind of assembly line consisting of mobile teams of workers who constructed one house and then moved to the next. It was, Levitt noted, like clockwork. "Eighteen houses completed on the shift from 8 to noon, and 18 more houses finished on the shift from 12:30 to 4:30."[4]

A section of houses in Levittown, New York, photographed in 1958

Levitt crews first flattened the existing land with a bulldozer and then laid concrete slabs. This meant that the houses would have no basements. Some families would miss having a basement, while others agreed that basements were damp, dark places used for storing things that were seldom used anyway. Street pavers followed, then electricians with light poles and men putting up street signs.

Convoys of trucks moved over the hardened pavement. Prefabricated sidings were erected, followed by flooring, sinks, bathtubs, and toilets. The exterior and interior of each house were painted by spray guns. Levitt built eight swimming pools for the community to enjoy, and land was set aside for schools, churches, and playgrounds.

According to Levitt's orders, nearly everything was uniform. Trees were planted 28 feet (8.5 m) apart. Levitt decreed that wash could be hung in backyards on Mondays, but under no circumstances would it be allowed to flap on clotheslines on Sundays. Picket fences were forbidden, and lawns had to be cut regularly.

Families who didn't want their houses to look like everyone else's were restricted to decorating only the inside differently. Also, since doorbells and buzzers were prohibited, Levitt householders had to use chimes (residents were allowed to vary the pitch of their chimes). To people who previously had lived in crowded city apartments or postwar Quonset huts and trailer camps, their new houses were no less enjoyable because they had been built according to standard specifications and rules laid down by Levitt.

After the first Levittown was completed, its creator acquired 8 square miles (21 square km) on the Delaware River in Pennsylvania. For Levittown II, there were 1,100 streets that had not only houses, schools, churches, and swimming pools, but also a shopping center, a railroad station, and baseball diamonds. Soon it had the tenth-largest population of any place in Pennsylvania. Levitt proudly called it "the most perfectly planned community in America."[5]

Builders throughout the country followed Levitt's lead, and new suburbs sprang up in many states. For example, in the

Picket fences

were

forbidden,

and lawns

had to be

cut regularly.

California suburb of Lakewood, near Long Beach, as many as one hundred houses were started each day, and 17,500 were completed in less than three years. "By 1955, *House and Garden* magazine reported that suburbia had become 'the national way of life.'"[6]

Many Americans, however, did not have the opportunity to experience life in the new suburbs. Some of them were rejected because they were African American or other minorities. Other people were too poor to make the move, or they had to remain in the cities to keep their jobs. Large numbers of urban dwellers continued to live in crowded cities, and many farmers had to stay where they tilled the land.

NEW ADVANCES IN TRANSPORTATION

The production and sale of automobiles increased phenomenally in the fifties. Beginning in 1950 and continuing for the rest of the decade, about 8 million cars were built every year.

By 1958, about 68 million cars and trucks were in use, including more than one automobile for every household.

Manufacturers turned out cars that were larger, fancier, and faster than earlier models. Soaring tail fins, giant headlights, and lots of chrome became standard features.

Elegant Oldsmobiles and the new Packards that were advertised as having the world's most powerful V-8 engines were popular. But heading the list of cars intended for elite buyers were Cadillacs, which had the longest tail fins. An ad for this car said that "at a conservative estimate, fifty percent of all the motorists in America would rather own a Cadillac than any other automobile."[7] The most expensive Cadillac was the El Dorado Brougham, which sold for about $14,000. It was fitted with a perfume bottle, a vanity case including lipsticks, a tissue dispenser on the dashboard, and four gold-finished drinking cups.

Fast sports cars appealed to many people, especially the younger generation. The Chevrolet Corvette, which was introduced in 1953, became a favorite attraction. The low, sleek, racy-looking Corvette coupe was likened by some enthusiasts to a flying saucer that had landed.

The 1953 Cadillac El Dorado, shown here in the convertible model, was the epitome of fifties car design and luxury.

The first 53-mile (85-km) section of the New Jersey Turnpike, which was one of the many highways constructed during the 1950s, was open for travel on November 5, 1951.

Beginning in the mid-1950s, some customers began turning to smaller cars that cost less, got better mileage, and were easier to park. Germany's Volkswagen (VW) Beetle led in this field. VW sales by 1957 were nearing the mark of 200,000. Soon, American car manufacturers were also producing small compact cars.

The National Defense Highway Act of 1956 was a great boon to auto travelers. This act provided for the construction of 41,000 miles (66,000 km) of freeways and highways to be built over a ten-year period at a cost of $26 billion. It was one of the largest public building projects in the history of the United States.

Driving swiftly along the new freeways without having to halt for numerous stoplights opened vast opportunities to many people. In a relatively short time, they could visit faraway relatives and friends or travel to historic sites and national parks, perhaps for the first time. The freeways spurred the growth of the oil, steel, and rubber industries; motels and hotels; gas stations; fast-food restaurants; and amusement centers such as Disneyland in Southern California, which opened in 1955.

There was major progress in the aviation industry, too. Jet planes had previously been used by the armed forces, but the first U.S. commercial jet airliner flew on December 10, 1958, from New York City to Miami, Florida. Soon, other jet planes were flying to many parts of the nation and across oceans to foreign destinations. These swift aircraft often cut in half the flying time between airports. Jets streaked across the continent in four and one-half hours and over the Atlantic Ocean in seven hours.

OTHER ACHIEVEMENTS

Traditionally, the Midwestern section of the United States had been handicapped in trade with Europe and other continents because of the great distance between these areas. But this problem was dealt with in the 1950s.

The St. Lawrence Seaway was jointly constructed by the United States and Canada. Work on it began in 1954, and it was opened by President Eisenhower and Queen Elizabeth II in 1959. The new seaway extended from the Gulf of Saint Lawrence in eastern Canada through the Great Lakes to the western end of Lake Superior. It enabled ships to journey 2,300 miles (3,701 km) from the Atlantic Ocean into the center of the continent. Fifteen locks lifted ships about 600 feet (183 m) above sea level by the time they reached Lake Superior.

The waterway linked more than fifty port cities with faraway destinations. Cities on the shores of the Great Lakes that produced metal ore and manufactured goods, as well as processed farm products from surrounding areas, were able to trade with a large market.

Medical science also made great progress in the 1950s. Penicillin, an antibiotic discovered in 1941, was used widely in the fifties. By the mid-1950s, scientists had introduced many other antibiotics that were used in treating such diseases as pneumonia, tuberculosis, and rheumatic fever. Other medical accomplishments included kidney transplants, cancer research, the use of laser beams in surgery, and the production of synthetic DNA.

One of the decade's most remarkable medical achievements pertained to poliomyelitis (polio). For many years polio had killed or crippled more youngsters than any other communicable disease, and many parents forbade their children from swimming in municipal pools or attending crowded events for fear their children would catch the dreaded disease.

Dr. Jonas Salk discovered a polio vaccine in 1954, and the following year it was declared safe and effective. Only 910 polio cases were reported in 1962, an amazing decrease from 37,476 in 1954. The virtual conquest of this disease was a victory of enormous importance.

Another new development in the 1950s was the addition of two more states to the Union. Both Alaska and Hawaii had been U.S. territories for many years, and in 1959, Congress made them states. They became the only states that did not border the continental United States, and Hawaii was the only state whose population was largely of Asian descent.

The flag-making industry soon had many orders to fill when the United States changed from forty-eight to fifty states, adding the new stars to its flag.

SEVEN

Television Takes Center Stage

Although experimental television broadcasts were being made as early as the 1920s, it was not until well after World War II that the TV industry really came to life. A Gallup poll in 1945 found that only 19 percent of Americans had actually seen a television show. As late as 1947, TV manufacturers produced fewer than 200,000 sets a year. By contrast, in the 1950s, manufacturers turned out six to seven million sets a year. This was the first decade when television really flourished.

As the 1950s started, there were some TV problems that still had to be resolved. Only a small number of cities had more than one station. The networks would sometimes coordinate efforts to screen a large event such as the World Series or a heavyweight boxing championship.

The technical obstacle to nationwide television remained: TV beams do not bend, and the curvature of the Earth's surface prevented television receivers across the country from picking up a station's picture. Because of this, program directors were limited to showing only local programs. This problem was solved in 1951 when a coaxial cable (a tube containing a central electrical conductor surrounded by conducting material that transmits high-frequency signals) was stretched across the United States. The first coast-to-coast television broadcast was President Truman's speech at the Japanese Peace Treaty Conference on September 4, 1951, which was beamed to 40 million viewers by ninety-four stations.

Some people criticized TV, calling it the "idiot box" or the "boob tube," claiming that many shows had little value. They objected to the violence and sex that often were depicted. It was estimated that in the single year of 1954, more people were murdered on TV than the United States lost in the entire Korean War.

The critics, however, were far outnumbered by the many Americans who greatly enjoyed TV programs. They didn't want to miss one minute of their favorite shows. Historian David Halberstam said, "Studies showed that when a popular program was on, toilets flushed all over certain cities, as if on cue, during commercials or the moment the program was over."[1]

The television revolution caused significant changes in lifestyle. Viewers tended to stay up later at night and leave home less often. Restaurants were more crowded during early night hours, so people could get back to the "tube" for the evening shows. Products advertised on TV, such as refrigerators and washing machines, soared in public acceptance. With the appearance of the TV dinner in 1954, dinnertime conversation became a lost art in some families. The ancestors of the frozen dinners we have today, TV dinners were given that name because their portability allowed them to be eaten while sitting in front of the television.

Radio programs and especially motion pictures were hit hard by the power of television. Many movie theaters began to close because attendance fell off sharply. In New York City, 55 movie theaters had closed by 1951, and in the same year in Southern California, the figure of shut-down movie houses stood at 134.

THE ZANY COMEDIANS

Milton Berle became television's first superstar. From his first appearance on TV in 1948, he caused his audience to howl with laughter. On his show, *Texaco Star Theater,* he brought vaudeville into the family living room. Berle did all sorts of funny things—don a dress and wig to appear as Cleopatra or Carmen Miranda, wear false teeth and rumpled clothing as a tough guy, become an organ grinder, and fall on his face or take a pie in it. Known as "Mr. Television" and "Uncle Miltie," Berle's fame was so great that his face was on the covers of both *Time* and *Newsweek* in the same week. In November 1948, NBC delayed the broadcast of the Truman-Dewey presidential race until Berle's program ended.

The show featuring Sid Caesar and Imogene Coca was another hit. This comedic pair were well known for their spoofs, such as that they did on Rudolph Valentino's romantic movie, *The Sheik*, and "From Here to Obscurity," a hilarious imitation of the film *From Here to Eternity*. Another funny show was Jackie Gleason's *The Honeymooners*.

Radio had been the chief form of home entertainment before the emergence of TV, and soon some of radio's stellar comedians turned their talents to television. The *Colgate Comedy Hour* boasted hosts such as Eddie Cantor, Abbott and Costello, and Dean Martin and Jerry Lewis. Other shows featured Jack Benny, Red Skelton, Jimmy Durante, and straight man George Burns with his scatterbrained wife, Gracie Allen. Charmed when they had heard Jimmy Durante on the radio wish Mrs. Calabash a good night (wherever she was), or listened to George Burns end his show with "Say good night, Gracie," fans relished these same lines on TV.

Newspaper columnist Ed Sullivan became the host of *Toast of the Town*, a popular variety show. It featured comedy acts, magicians, sports players, and singers, including the teenagers' idol, Elvis Presley. There were so many different types of performers that a mimic named Will Jordan once went on a program doing an imitation of Sullivan and said, "Tonight on our really big show we have 702 Polish dentists who will be here in a few moments doing their marvelous extractions."[2]

The biggest comedy hit of the 1950s was *I Love Lucy*, which premiered on Monday, October 15, 1951. It featured wacky Lucille Ball and her Cuban-born bandleader husband, Desi Arnaz. At the end of its first month, *I Love Lucy* displaced Milton Berle's show as the top-rated TV program. Less than a year later, its stars signed a new contract for $8 million, which at that time was the largest amount paid any television performers. More people watched *I Love Lucy* in January 1953 than saw President Eisenhower's inauguration in the same month, and by 1954, 50 million people were Lucy and Desi's devoted fans.

The first episode showed Desi wanting to go to a prizefight and arranging for a blind date. Lucy learned of his plan, dressed in an outlandish costume that included a wig, and posed as his blind date without him recognizing her. Later humorous episodes found Lucy working in a factory and doing everything wrong, trying to make wine by crushing grapes with her feet, shoving too many marshmallows into her mouth, and being slapped in the face with a pie.

A problem arose when Lucy discovered she was pregnant with her second child. In those times, pregnant women had not been seen on television or in films because this was considered to be in poor taste. Lucy and Desi delivered the news to Jess Oppenheimer, their producer and head writer. Unfazed, Oppenheimer immediately shouted, "What a gimmick! I've been wondering what we were going to do next season!"[3]

Week after week the nation watched with fascination as Lucy's stomach grew larger and larger. Lucy was serene as she waited for the big event, but Desi was so nervous that one scene showed him arriving at the hospital with Lucy pushing him in a wheelchair. When the baby was delivered, people throughout the country heaved a sigh of relief.

FAMILY FARE FOR MANY TASTES

There were so many types of TV shows in the 1950s that virtually everyone could find something interesting to watch. For fans who enjoyed spectacular programs, the top attraction of the decade was the first television broadcast of a Broadway production, *Peter Pan*. In this show, Mary Martin played Peter, and she flew gracefully through the air suspended on wires. It was said that one out of every two Americans watched this brilliant presentation.

Ozzie and Harriet, beginning in 1952, was the country's favorite family show. It featured scripts written by Ozzie Nelson that were drawn from and acted by his real family. The program ran for fourteen seasons, long enough for both of Ozzie and Harriet's sons to grow up and get married and for younger brother Ricky to become a singing star. The week after Ricky sang "I'm Walkin'" on the show, a million copies of his recording were sold.

Among the other popular family shows were *Father Knows Best*, *Our Miss Brooks*, *Make Room for Daddy*, and *Leave It to Beaver*. These shows portrayed an idealized version of American society and American families where problems were solved more quickly and easily than in real life. Many families aspired to be like the TV families, but few actually were.

For fans of Westerns there were many programs to choose from. These included *King of the Cowboys*, starring Roy Rogers and his wife, Dale Evans, and *Zorro*, featuring a mysterious avenger of evil doings who would thunder off in the night leaving only a telltale "Z" to mark his passing. Other well-received Westerns were *Wyatt Earp*; *Have Gun, Will Travel*; *The Rifleman*; *Wagon Train*; *The Cisco Kid*; and *Cheyenne*.

The most popular Western was *Gunsmoke*, which premiered on September 10, 1955. "Its main character, Marshal Matt Dillon, wasn't the quickest draw in Dodge City, but he was a sure shot, and his individualism and rough decency mirrored commonly held notions about what it was that made America great."[4]

Some people believed that the many cowboy sagas created a televised form of literature. One actor said, "If Shakespeare were alive today, he'd be writing Westerns."[5]

The most widely watched detective program on TV was *Dragnet*. It was created by Jack Webb, who not only directed the show and wrote many of its scripts, but also played the role of crime-busting Sergeant Joe Friday. Each episode was

The cast of <u>Leave It to Beaver</u>. Theodore "Beaver" Cleaver, played by actor Jerry Mathers, is at lower right.

based on an actual case from the Los Angeles Police Department files. *Perry Mason* and *Alfred Hitchcock Presents* were other popular mystery and suspense programs.

The 1950s provided some of the best live plays ever written for television. Advertisers supported these hour-long shows produced on such programs as *Philco Playhouse*, *Kraft Television Theater*, and the *U.S. Steel Hour*.

Paddy Chayefsky's TV play *Marty*, about a lonely, awkward man, was a smashing success. Chayefsky later expanded his hour-long script into a full-length film, which won the 1955 Academy Award for the best movie of the year.

Rod Serling's *Requiem for a Heavyweight* tells the story of a defeated boxer who feels he has nothing left except his own self-respect. It is such a moving story that it is still shown in theaters today.

Music also had a place on television. Disc jockey Dick Clark on *American Bandstand* had 20 million regular viewers and kept teenagers apprised of the latest songs. Van Cliburn played the piano masterfully on television. Many singers of popular songs lent their talents to the "tube."

Amahl and the Night Visitors by Gian-Carlo Menotti in 1951 became the first opera ever written for television. It was so successful that it has been performed in many opera houses. Soon TV viewers were able to enjoy many other operas.

Television did not overlook children's shows. These included the popular *Kukla, Fran and Ollie*. When the show finally ended in 1957, even presidential candidate Adlai Stevenson was dismayed. He sadly observed, "For reasons incomprehensible to me this charming bit of satire . . . and fantasy is about to go off the air. Surely such an assassination cannot be permitted in this enlightened land of culture and sophistication."[6]

Other popular children's programs were *Captain Kangaroo*, *Howdy Doody*, *Mighty Mouse Playhouse*, and *Lassie*, the dog that captured the hearts of nearly every youngster who watched her perform. And thousands of small boys wore coonskin caps in tribute to their television hero, Davy Crockett.

QUIZ SHOWS AND SCANDALS

Quiz shows became a TV phenomenon in the 1950s. Americans were fascinated by the idea of ordinary people competing for self-made riches. "Into the vacated myth of quick success," one writer declared, "the jackpot quiz shows came with an answer. They came to an audience hungry for glory, excitement, surprises and reassurance that the man in the anonymous street might still suddenly rise to a place in the golden sun."[7]

You Bet Your Life, featuring comedian Groucho Marx, was introduced in 1950. In addition to paying money for correct answers during a quiz portion of the show, it awarded $100 to the person who happened to use the day's secret word, at which time an artificial duck dropped from the ceiling. The audience loved the funny remarks of cigar-chewing Marx.

What's My Line? was another early quiz show, and it lasted for more than seventeen years. Hosted by John Daly, the show consisted of four panelists who asked many questions in order to guess the occupation of a contestant who signed in on a blackboard telling the audience what he or she did for a living. The occupations were difficult to figure out, such as putting holes in doughnuts, selling church steeples, and polishing jelly beans.

The first quiz show to offer a large amount of money was *The $64,000 Question*. Contestants had to answer a series of questions based on a single topic while enclosed in an isolation booth. As many as 20,000 people a week wrote to the producers pleading for a chance to appear on the show and possibly win a big cash prize. Psychologist Dr. Joyce Brothers became famous by answering questions about boxing and winning $64,000. Soon there were other big-money quiz shows, including *Twenty-One*, *Tic Tac Dough*, and *Beat the Jackpot*.

The program *Twenty-One* attracted a large audience but suffered a scandalous fate. On *Twenty-One*, two players competed against each other to score twenty-one points by answering questions of increasing difficulty that were worth increasing amounts of money.

"I would give

almost

anything I

have to

reverse the

course of my

life in the

last three

years. . . ."

Charles Van Doren was a handsome young man earning $4,400 a year as a Columbia University instructor, and he came from a famous literary family. When he appeared on *Twenty-One*, he became very good at performing the theatrical gestures that the show required to increase its dramatic impact. He learned how to stutter, stammer, and even sweat in the camera's limelight. He amazed 25 million viewers by being able to name the only three baseball players who had collected more than 3,500 hits, identify opera arias, and give the names of Snow White's seven dwarfs, pausing dramatically before revealing the last one, Bashful.

Van Doren amassed a record payoff of $129,000 and became an instant celebrity. But his fame turned to shame. Herbert Stempel, a college student who had won $49,500 on the show in 1956, wanted revenge because the producers of *Twenty-One* had ordered him to miss a question and lose to Van Doren. Stempel revealed to the press that all the contestants were given the correct answers in advance and continued to win money until their popularity waned. He told the reporters that the entire show was a monstrous fake.

When Van Doren was confronted by Stempel's charges, at first he denied that he had been given the questions and answers before the show aired. However, a congressional committee investigated the matter and subpoenaed him to testify.

On November 2, 1959, a tense and forlorn Van Doren confessed to the congressional investigators that he previously had lied and that *Twenty-One* was indeed a fraud. He explained that when he kept winning, his conscience was troubled, and he had begged the producers several times to let him lose, but they refused.

Looking back to 1956 when he had been forced to defeat Stempel, Van Doren grimly said, "I would give almost anything I have to reverse the course of my life in the last three years. . . . I've learned a lot about good and evil. They are not always what they appear to be. I was involved, deeply involved in a deception. . . . I was almost able to convince myself that it did not matter what I was doing because it was having such a good effect on the national attitude toward teachers, education, and the intellectual life."[8]

Van Doren was not prosecuted for his misdeeds, but he slipped into obscurity. Some contestants on *The $64,000 Question* and other quiz programs also came forward and admitted that they had learned answers during rehearsals. By the end of the decade, the big-money quiz shows had faded from TV screens, and they remained dormant for many years.

NEWS AND PUBLIC EVENTS

The news programs on TV in the early 1950s lasted only fifteen minutes, but later they were extended to half an hour. Television news coverage became a living newspaper; people could actually see and hear the daily headlines. Soon, most Americans were relying more on television than on newspapers and radio for news.

The major news commentators were Edward R. Murrow at CBS, David Brinkley and Chet Huntley at NBC, and an ABC team headed by John Daly. In 1951, Murrow, who was well known for his outstanding radio broadcasts from Europe during World War II, launched a popular news show called *See It Now*, in which he covered events all over the world. Murrow said, "No journalistic age was ever given a weapon for truth with quite the scope of this fledgling television."[9]

Important public events also were covered by television. Viewers watched political conventions and elections, as well as some of the speeches given by presidential candidates Dwight Eisenhower and Adlai Stevenson. They also were intrigued by the televised hearings of Senator Joseph McCarthy's fight with the U.S. Army.

They saw on TV Senator Estes Kefauver's congressional hearings on organized crime in 1950 and Queen Elizabeth II's coronation in 1952. When Soviet Premier Nikita Khrushchev made an unprecedented visit to the United States in 1959, this, too, was widely covered by television cameras.

EIGHT

More Entertainment

There were countless ways to have fun in the fifties. Besides watching television, people could go to the movies, sometimes at drive-in theaters, followed by a snack at a drive-in restaurant. Or they could go to a dance or a concert, which for the younger generation usually meant a rock-and-roll concert. If people preferred to have a party at home, they could play the new 45-revolutions-per-minute records. Ten of these smaller records could be stacked on the spindle of a portable player, and the 45s could be bought for as little as sixty-nine cents apiece.

A bevy of new fads reflected the fun-loving spirit of the decade. One example was a rite called "stuffing" that swept across college campuses in the late 1950s. The idea was to cram many people into a small space. At St. Mary's College in California twenty-two young men squeezed into a public telephone booth. In Modesto, California, the telephone company set up a booth into which thirty-two students crammed themselves. This "sport" could even be done underwater; each of seven young men held his breath long enough to squeeze into a booth sunk in a swimming pool.

College students in Long Beach, California, were photographed "stuffing" a motorbike in April 1959.

In 1958, two California toy makers learned about gym classes in Australia where youngsters exercised with bamboo hoops, so they began manufacturing plastic rings called hula hoops. Within six months, American girls and boys were spinning 30 million hula hoops. At a hula hoop derby at a New Jersey swim club, a ten-year-old boy set the club record by completing three thousand spins.

People of all ages were attracted to another fad: using products made with chlorophyll, the green substance found in plants. Their manufacturers promised that those who used chlorophyll products would smell clean and fresh. Consumers bought large amounts of chlorophyll green toothpaste, deodorants, chewing gum, cough drops, and even canned food for dogs. This craze began to ease after the American Medical Association explained that grazing goats virtually live on chlorophyll and still smell bad.

Painting by number was an artistic fad in the 1950s. Professional artists created the paint kits and the numbered designs on which the paint was applied. By 1954, more "number paintings," based on such subjects as landscapes, seascapes, and portraits of famous persons, were hanging in American homes than original works of art. There also was a West Wing gallery in the White House of paint-by-number pictures done by government officials, including FBI director J. Edgar Hoover and New York political leader Nelson Rockefeller.

Many true artists condemned this artificial way to paint a picture. One concerned correspondent wrote, "I don't know what America is coming to when thousands of people, many of them adults, are willing to be regimented into brushing paint on a jig-saw miscellany of dictated shapes and all by rote. Can't you rescue some of these souls—or should I say 'morons'?—before they are lost forever?"[1] Nevertheless, fans of the fad would one day be avenged. In 2001, an exhibit called "Paint by Number: Accounting for Taste in the 1950s" opened at the National Museum of American History.

People also enjoyed the fashions of the fifties. Women's clothes ranged from the hooded dress made of a single tube of hip-clinging knit fabric to a skirt worn over a stiff crinoline petticoat that made the skirt very full. Hats and gloves were required for many social functions and going to church. Women not endowed with a large bosom made padded bra sales soar.

Girls often wore rolled-up jeans with casual blouses or men's shirts. Another favorite was a felt skirt on which was appliquéd an adorable poodle. Girls' hairstyles ranged from the ponytail and poodle cut to the bouffant look where most of the hair was puffed up on top of the head.

As the 1950s continued, many girls began wearing skimpy bikini swimsuits. This type of swimwear has been very common for many years, and almost no one is surprised or shocked by it today. But a half century ago, it was considered very daring. Some parents and many preachers called it scandalous. The same reaction had been expressed in the early 1900s when female swimmers cast aside bloomers that reached to their ankles and blouses that stretched to their necks. At that time, these confining, uncomfortable garments were replaced by one-piece swimsuits that revealed the wearer's legs, arms, and shoulders.

Two teenage girls try on crinolines over their shorts in Dearborn, Michigan, in July 1956.

Businessmen wore suits, ties, and always hats to and from the office. On weekends, they shed their more formal attire for colorful sport shirts and slacks or jeans.

The favorite casual dress of high school boys was either baggy pegged pants or denim jeans with rolled-up cuffs. Both T-shirts and sport shirts were regular attire. In 1955, teenage boys joined older males in college in what became known as the pink revolution. They donned pink shirts and pink striped or polka dot ties. At a dance it was hard to find any young men not wearing lots of pink with their gray flannel suits. Hairstyles ranged from the flattop and crew cut, which had been popular in the wartime 1940s, to the swooping ducktail worn by Elvis Presley.

Sporting 3-D glasses, this audience in Hollywood witnesses the first full-length 3-D movie, Bwana Devil, on November 26, 1952.

THE MOVIES

Hollywood tried various innovations to win back at least part of the huge audience it had lost to television. The search for technological improvements began in 1952 with the introduction of Cinerama. Using three projectors on a large screen, Cinerama made viewers feel that they were taking part in all the exciting action they saw. But the expense of revamping theaters with an extra-wide screen and acquiring the necessary equipment limited its possibilities.

Next came three-dimensional (3-D) movies, which involved the use of two projectors. Audiences had to watch 3-D films with special polarized glasses that gave the illusion of depth. However, most of the 3-D films were poorly scripted adventure stories, and this fad soon disappeared.

Producers at Twentieth Century Fox decided to gamble with a new projection method called Cinemascope that was able to compress a large picture area on a standard 35-millimeter frame. Referring to the need to wear cumbersome glasses for 3-D movies, the first Cinemascope ads proclaimed, "Thanks to this modern miracle you can see without the use of glasses."[2]

Released in 1953, *The Robe*, a story about what might have happened to Christ's robe, was the first Cinemascope film, and it was a huge box-office success. So was *The Ten Commandments* (1956), a biography of Moses.

The most colossal of these Cinemascope epics of the 1950s was *Ben Hur* (1959), starring Charlton Heston in the title role of a Jewish patriot in the early days of Christianity when Palestine was ruled by Rome. This extravagant movie was filmed on more than 300 sets with 10,000 extras, 100,000 costumes, and a million props. Costing $15 million—the most expensive movie yet produced—it earned more than $80 million and won eleven Academy Awards.

Technicolor made giant strides in the fifties. The attraction of viewing movies in all their vibrant colors, instead of in only black and white, drew millions of people back to theaters.

There were sensational new movie stars in the 1950s. Heading the list was Marilyn Monroe, the sex symbol of the decade. She usually was cast in the role of a voluptuous, naïve blonde constantly being pursued by a throng of adoring men. Monroe achieved worldwide fame in *Gentlemen Prefer Blondes* (1953), and when she appeared at its first showing, scores of males rushed through theater doors to watch her depart. Her huge box-office hits also included *The Seven Year Itch* (1955), *Bus Stop* (1956), and *Some Like It Hot* (1959).

Monroe received five thousand fan letters a week, and when she visited Japan, people fell into fishponds trying to get a glimpse of her. But the popular actress, who once was married to Joe DiMaggio, the New York Yankees' premier player, and later to playwright Arthur Miller, was very confused by and unhappy with her public image, which had become almost impossible to control. She once said, "Sometimes [fame] makes you a little bit sad because you'd like to meet somebody kind of on face value. It's nice to be included in people's fantasies, but you also like to be accepted for your own sake."[3]

Elizabeth Taylor was another rising star in the fifties. In 1951's *A Place in the Sun*, the seventeen-year-old violet-eyed beauty played a pampered society girl whose romance with a handsome poor man ends catastrophically. Taylor also was praised for superb performances in *Giant* (1956), and *Cat on a Hot Tin Roof* (1958).

The most regal of the new feminine stars, Grace Kelly, the daughter of a wealthy Philadelphia family, brought heightened sophistication and elegance to the screen. Alfred Hitchcock directed her in three thrillers: *Dial M for Murder* and *Rear Window*, both in 1954, and *To Catch a Thief* (1955). She proved the breadth of her acting talent when she gave up her fashionable clothes to portray a dowdy, lower-class wife in *The Country Girl* (1954), for which she won a Best Actress Academy Award. In 1956, Kelly retired from films and became a princess when she married Prince Rainier III of tiny Monaco.

Actress Grace Kelly is surrounded by fans and photographers on a street in New York City on March 30, 1956.

One of the new leading male actors who achieved fame in the 1950s was Marlon Brando. He had starred in *A Streetcar Named Desire* on the Broadway stage and in 1951 performed the same role on the screen. A film historian declared, "Overnight a new Hollywood white hope was born. . . . The young man's combined savagery and inarticulateness struck flaring responses in teenagers, to whom they reflected their own frustration at a society they could not understand or participate in."[4]

Virile Brando made several other box-office hits in the 1950s. These included *Viva Zapata* (1952), *The Wild One* (1953), *On the Waterfront* and *Desiree*, both in 1954, *Guys and Dolls* (1955), *The Teahouse of the August Moon* (1956), *Sayonara* (1957), and *The Young Lions* (1958).

James Dean was an actor who had a spectacular but brief career in movies. In his only year in Hollywood, 1955, this handsome, moody Indiana farm boy with a sensitivity and capacity to express emotions distinctly his own, starred in three films that had enormous appeal to teenagers: *East of Eden*, *Rebel Without a Cause*, and *Giant*. A week after he completed *Giant*, Dean died in an automobile accident, a loss "which enshrined him forever as the idol and symbol of a restless, confused, but fundamentally idealistic younger generation."[5]

Besides the newcomers, Hollywood's veteran actors made some outstanding movies in the fifties. Gary Cooper starred in *High Noon* (1952), perhaps the best Western movie ever made. After many years of absence, aging Gloria Swanson came back to the screen in *Sunset Boulevard* (1950). She played the role of a forgotten star slowly moving toward madness as she broods over her vanished fame. Bette Davis starred in *All About Eve* (1950), and Judy Garland was superb in *A Star Is Born* (1954). Katharine Hepburn and Humphrey Bogart achieved great success together in *The African Queen* (1951).

Science-fiction films were popular in the fifties. *Destination Moon* (1950) was the first major movie about the possibility of lunar exploration, shown nineteen years before this spectacular mission was accomplished. In *The Day the Earth Stood Still* (1951), a spaceman and a robot land in Washington, D.C., in a flying saucer, and unless the spaceman's order to quit using atomic bombs is followed, the robot will use such weapons to destroy Earth. Other major science-fiction movies were *Invasion of the Body Snatchers* (1956), *The Incredible Shrinking Man* (1957), and *On the Beach* (1959). Many of these movies reflected the public's fear of nuclear annihilation.

THE STAGE

Live theater had much to cheer about in the fifties. Perhaps no other decade offered more great musicals and serious plays. Even though they are more than half a century old, many of them are still being shown on stages today.

Guys and Dolls (1950) was the first smash musical hit of the decade. It featured New York gamblers and their girlfriends and provided such memorable songs as "Sit Down, You're

Rockin' the Boat" and "Luck Be a Lady." The next year, Broadway audiences raved about Richard Rodgers and Oscar Hammerstein's *The King and I*, which tells about the relationship that develops between the strong-willed king of Siam and the British governess he hires to teach his many children.

The biggest single musical hit of the decade was *My Fair Lady* by Alan Lerner and Frederick Loewe. It opened in 1956 and had 2,717 consecutive performances, breaking all previous records for Broadway musicals. Starring Rex Harrison as Professor Henry Higgins and Julie Andrews as a young, poor flower seller, it is the story of how this erudite professor teaches a woman with a strong cockney accent to speak like a lady.

Meredith Willson's *The Music Man* (1957) delighted Broadway theatergoers, who went home humming the invigorating song "Seventy-Six Trombones." Robert Preston starred as a fast-talking huckster who travels the Midwest peddling brass band instruments to small-town customers.

Based on Shakespeare's *Romeo and Juliet*, *West Side Story* opened in 1957. Set in New York City, it tells the tale of young lovers caught in a feud between rival gangs. Leonard Bernstein wrote the music for *West Side Story*, which had many beautiful songs and spectacular dances.

The last great musical of the decade was Rodgers and Hammerstein's *The Sound of Music* (1959). Featuring Mary Martin as the governess of a wealthy Austrian's children, it ran on Broadway for nearly four years, and audiences loved its warmth and many fine songs. When Julie Andrews played the same role in the movie, *The Sound of Music* was enhanced by breathtaking scenes of the Austrian Alps, and in 1965 this film won the Academy Award as the year's best picture.

Some outstanding nonmusical plays debuted in the decade. New playwright William Inge provided four plays that drew large audiences: *Come Back, Little Sheba*, and *Picnic* (1953), *Bus Stop* (1954), and *The Dark at the Top of the Stairs* (1957). Tennessee Williams wrote a trio of box-office hits, *The Rose Tattoo* (1951), *Cat on a Hot Tin Roof* (1954), and *Sweet Bird of Youth* (1958).

Arthur Miller's *The Crucible* was first performed in 1953. Set in colonial times, it tells about people who accuse their neighbors of being witches and reminded audiences of McCarthy's "witchhunts." In the same year John Patrick's delightful *The Teahouse of the August Moon* was staged. The following year offered Agatha Christie's thriller, *Witness for the Prosecution*.

Inherit the Wind, the story of the landmark Scopes trial that discusses whether evolution should be taught in public schools, opened in 1955. In that year, another powerful play was *The Diary of Anne Frank*. It tells the now-famous story of a teenage Jewish girl whose entire family is killed by the Nazis during World War II.

Eugene O'Neill's serious *Long Day's Journey into Night* premiered in 1956, as did a play on the lighter side, *Auntie Mame*. Rosalind Russell played the eccentric Mame.

Based on Thomas Wolfe's powerful novel, *Look Homeward, Angel* appeared in 1957. The story of Franklin D. Roosevelt's fight against polio, *Sunrise at Campobello*, premiered in 1958. The next year audiences saw a play about another person overcoming physical handicaps, Helen Keller, whose tale was told in *The Miracle Worker*. Also in 1959, a remarkable play about a black family reached Broadway. It was *A Raisin in the Sun*, which starred Sidney Poitier and Claudia McNeil.

MUSIC

Popular music in the early 1950s was much as it had been in the previous decade. Blanketing the nation were romantic ballads by such vocalists as Perry Como, Eddie Fisher, Harry Belafonte, Nat King Cole, Patti Page, Kay Starr, Teresa Brewer, Rosemary Clooney, and the Andrews Sisters. Youngsters jitterbugged to Teresa Brewer's "Music! Music! Music!" and Rosemary Clooney's "Come On-a My House."

A revolution, however, was brewing in the world of popular music. The younger generation was taken by storm by the introduction of rock and roll. It was a combination of rhythm and blues from the South and so-called hillbilly (country) music, which was another Southern musical tradition.

Bill Haley and his Comets became one of the first groups to be labeled rock and rollers. Their "Rock Around the Clock" (1955) was a smash hit. Chuck Berry blended hillbilly with rhythm and blues in "Maybelline," also in 1955, and Berry soon was the most important black performer of early rock and roll.

The towering idol of rock and roll was Elvis Presley, a former Memphis, Tennessee, truck driver who wore pegged pants and had a ducktail haircut with long sideburns. Presley strummed a guitar and swiveled his hips suggestively wherever he performed.

With the 1956 release of such records as "Heartbreak Hotel," "Hound Dog," and "Don't Be Cruel," Presley became an overnight sensation. "Heartbreak Hotel" was the number-one hit, while "Don't Be Cruel" sold three million copies and "Hound Dog" two million copies. In 1957, due largely to Presley's influence, rock accounted for two-thirds of the sixty best-selling records in the United States.

Presley was so adored by the younger generation that at one concert a mob of girls broke through police lines backstage, and before he got away they stripped him of his coat, shirt, and shoes. But Elvis had grown accustomed to such treatment, and he said, "Sure they tear off my clothes, they scratch their initials on my cars, they phone my hotel all night. . . . When they stop, I'll start to worry."[6]

Some adults were outraged by rock and roll. FBI director J. Edgar Hoover called it "a menace to morals."[7] A spokesman for the White Citizens' Council in Alabama called it a plot to mongrelize Americans because rock and roll appealed to both whites and blacks. The city of Boston even banned rock concerts temporarily after several were disrupted by violent incidents. But an Arizona high school student struck back, saying, "Man, I believe the older generation just doesn't want the younger generation to have any fun."[8]

Nobody had ever seen anything like Elvis Presley before. He was photographed during an August 1956 concert in Jacksonville, Florida.

Today we are surprised by all this commotion regarding rock-and-roll music. Presley is considered one of the greatest popular singers ever to perform, and every year thousands of people visit Graceland, his home in Memphis, Tennessee. Music fans of all ages continue to enjoy rock and roll. But in the 1950s, the situation was different. Presley, with his sexually charged performances, offended some people. However, after Elvis had appeared three times on Ed Sullivan's popular television show, Sullivan told his audience, "I want to say to Elvis Presley and the country that this is a real decent, fine boy. We've never had a pleasanter experience on our show with a big name than we've had with you. You're all right."[9]

Classical music had some important achievements in the 1950s. Marian Anderson became the first black singer to play a leading role at the Metropolitan Opera House when she appeared in *Un Ballo in Maschera* (1955). In the same year the very successful black *Porgy and Bess* was the first American opera to be performed at the famous La Scala Opera House in Milan, Italy.

In 1956, a fiery soprano of Greek heritage, Maria Callas, sang for the first time at the Metropolitan in the opera *Norma*, and her appearance grossed a record $75,510. Also in 1956, Beverly Sills, who later became one of America's favorite opera singers, made her debut in *The Ballad of Baby Doe* in Colorado.

Twenty-three-year-old Van Cliburn won first prize at the International Tchaikovsky Piano Competition in 1958. This brought him instant fame, including a ticker-tape parade in New York City.

Among the decade's most prominent composers were Aaron Copland, Leonard Bernstein, Roy Harris, and John Cage. Some of the musical performances were not of a serious nature. President Truman played the piano and comedian Jack Benny the violin in a 1958 benefit performance with the Kansas City Philharmonic Orchestra.

LITERATURE

Many people thought that the new popularity of television would greatly reduce the sale of books, but they were wrong. In the 1950s, 53 percent more books were sold than in the 1940s.

Military themes were highlighted in some of the best-sellers, partly because readers linked them to their ongoing concerns about the Cold War. *From Here to Eternity* (1951), by James Jones, tells about army life in Hawaii. Herman Wouk's *The Caine Mutiny* (1954) depicts the rebellion of a disgruntled naval crew against their unbalanced Captain Queeg.

Ernest Hemingway wrote *The Old Man and the Sea* (1952), the story of an aged Cuban fisherman's struggle against a huge fish. This short book won Hemingway the Nobel Prize for literature in 1954.

One of the best-selling books of the decade was *Peyton Place* (1956), by Grace Metalious. It depicts the many scandals that occur in what appears to be a staid New England town.

J. D. Salinger's *The Catcher in the Rye* was published in 1956. Its chief characters are sensitive youngsters who feel trapped in a conformist world, and the book had a strong appeal to teenage readers.

Two writers, Jack Kerouac and Allen Ginsberg, became early literary leaders of the so-called Beat Generation. In his 1957 best-seller, *On the Road,* Kerouac struck out fiercely against current culture and lifestyles. Poet Ginsberg did the same in "Howl," which he first read in 1955. There was a powerful link between the Beats of the 1950s and the dissatisfied hippies of the 1960s.

In 1958, a fascinating account of the Communist revolution in Russia was Boris Pasternak's *Doctor Zhivago,* which later was made into a lengthy and successful movie. The following year Leon Uris's *Exodus* dealt with the important story of the birth of Israel. In a single year, *Doctor Zhivago* sold 500,000 copies and *Exodus* sold 400,000 copies.

Among the most prominent nonfiction books in the fifties were a Revised Standard Version of the Bible, which led all sales in 1952 through 1954; Anne Morrow Lindbergh's *Gift from the Sea* (1955); Norman Vincent Peale's *The Power of Positive Thinking* (1955); and Betty Crocker's *Picture Cook Book* (1956).

Several popular magazines made their debuts in the 1950s. They included *Mad, Sports Illustrated, Playboy,* and *TV Guide.*

ART AND ARCHITECTURE

In the 1950s, abstract art took center stage. Jackson Pollock was the chief leader of this movement. He defied the long-standing traditions of art and saw painting as a means of total personal expression. His 18-foot (5-m)-wide *Blue Poles,* painted in 1952, resulted in widespread approval by many art critics.

Pollack dripped paint on the canvas with a stick or sometimes splattered it directly from a can. Many viewers who did not understand Pollock's work thought it was ridiculous and labeled the artist "Jack the Dripper." Pollock defended what he painted, saying, "It's just like looking at a bed of flowers. You don't tear your hair out over what it means."[10] His importance continued to grow, and in 1960 a Pollock painting sold for $100,000.

Robert Rauschenberg was another artist who was a nonconformist. For his artworks he used not only paint but also such objects as parts of ladders, automobile tires, rags, Coke bottles, old radios, and newspaper clippings.

Many sculptors also belonged to the abstractionist school and used various materials and experimented with new shapes. By hammering, twisting, or welding steel and bronze, outstanding forms of sculpture emerged.

There still were traditional artists in the 1950s, such as Andrew Wyeth, Georgia O'Keeffe, and Anna "Grandma"

Moses, who started painting at age seventy-eight. Moses's paintings were exhibited all over the nation and reproduced on fabrics, china, and many greeting cards.

There were some remarkable architectural accomplishments in the 1950s. The United Nation headquarters in New York City was designed by three prominent architects in 1950. Richard Neutra created the Hinds House in Los Angeles in 1952 and the Navy Chapel at Miramar, California, in 1956. In 1953, Buckminster Fuller designed the Ford Rotunda at Dearborn, Michigan, and the Mini-Earth Sphere Geoscope at Ithaca, New York.

The most prominent architect of the fifties was Frank Lloyd Wright. He designed the First Unitarian Meeting House in Madison, Wisconsin, and the Wayfarers Chapel in Palos Verdes, California, both in 1951. He drew the plans for the Price Tower in Bartlesville, Oklahoma, in 1955, and both the Beth Sholom Synagogue in Elkins Park, Pennsylvania, and the Kalita Humphreys Theater in Dallas, Texas, in 1959.

Perhaps Wright's most notable achievement in the 1950s was the Solomon R. Guggenheim Museum on New York City's Fifth Avenue. It was begun in 1958 and completed in 1959 after Wright's death. A conch shell inspired Wright's design for the museum's exhibition galleries. Shaped like a large cone, it includs a sloping ramp that spirals down for seven stories beneath a huge glass dome.

Architect Frank Lloyd Wright's Solomon R. Guggenheim Museum in New York City

Bobby Thomson (with his head being rubbed) is mobbed by his New York Giants teammates after hitting a three-run homer in the bottom of the ninth inning in the third game of the National League championship against the Brooklyn Dodgers on October 3, 1951.

NINE

A Golden Age of Sports

More leisure time was available in the 1950s. Modern conveniences, including improved means of transportation, reduced the time needed to travel between home and work sites. Housewives now had the time to take part in many outdoor activities. People of all ages were able to spend longer periods playing and enjoying sports. But the decade's biggest change in the world of sports was that television now brought all types of sporting events into family homes. At first it was feared that this would reduce attendance at these events. Instead, the opposite was true. Fans became more attracted to favorite teams and athletic heroes, so they paid record amounts of money to watch them play in person.

BASEBALL

Experts generally agree that baseball's greatest single game, capping the most fantastic comeback of any major league team, occurred in 1951. On August 12, as the season was nearing its end, the Brooklyn Dodgers led the New York Giants by a seemingly insurmountable thirteen and one-half games. But the Giants surged in the closing weeks of the season, winning thirty-seven of their last forty-four games, including sixteen in a row.

On the last day of the regular season, the two teams were tied for first place. For only the second time in National League history, a two-out-of-three-games playoff would decide the championship.

The Giants won the first game, the Dodgers the second. Everything now depended on the third game. The entire nation was caught up in the drama. Fans stood in the streets to watch television sets in store windows. The Dow Jones stock reports were interrupted for the play-by-play account. Announcers at racetracks provided more coverage to the game than they did to which horses were winning races, and many prison inmates were allowed to postpone other duties so they could watch the game on TV.

Brooklyn was leading 4–2 in the last half of the ninth inning and appeared headed for victory. Two Giants were on base when tall, lanky third baseman Bobby Thomson came to the plate. He took the first pitch for a strike, but he hit a home run on the next pitch, giving New York a 5-4 win and the National League pennant.

Russ Hodges, broadcasting the game, verged on hysteria. Three times he screamed, "The Giants win the pennant!" Then he added, "Bobby Thomson hits it into the lower decks of the left field stands. . . . They're going crazy! I don't believe it"[1]

"The art of fiction is dead," wrote an excited Red Smith after the game. "Reality has strangled invention. Only the utterly impossible, the inexpressibly fantastic, can ever be plausible again."[2]

The amazing Giants lost the World Series to the New York Yankees, but this was not surprising. The Yankees were the dominant baseball team in the 1950s, winning eight American League pennants and six World Series.

The Yankees' manager was Casey Stengel, who was well known for his unorthodox remarks and fractured English. Once he said, "All right, everybody line up alphabetically according to your height"; and another time he declared, "I'd always heard it couldn't be done, but sometimes it don't always work."[3]

Yankee superstar Joe DiMaggio retired from baseball in 1951. He had a lifetime batting average of .325, had hit 361 home runs, and had an apparently unbeatable record of making at least one hit in fifty-six consecutive games.

Di Maggio was replaced in the outfield by Mickey Mantle, who became one of the game's most powerful sluggers, hitting 536 home runs in his colorful career. Other fabulous Yankees in the fifties included catcher Yogi Berra, second baseman Billy Martin, and pitchers Whitey Ford and Don Larsen. In 1956, Larsen pitched the only perfect game in World Series history, allowing no hits, no walks, and no runs.

Among the many non-Yankees who were great players in the 1950s were pitcher Bob Lemon of the Cleveland Indians, and outfielders Stan Musial of the St. Louis Cardinals, Ted Williams of the Boston Red Sox, "Duke" Snider of the Brooklyn Dodgers, and Al Kaline of the Detroit Tigers.

One of the most important baseball developments was the introduction of black players into the major leagues. Jackie Robinson was the first African American to break the color line when the Brooklyn Dodgers hired him in 1947. Over a ten-year period, Robinson batted .311, played five positions, stole many bases, and qualified for baseball's prestigious Hall of Fame at Cooperstown, New York.

Groundbreaking baseball wonder Jackie Robinson poses for an action shot in 1951.

Soon there were other outstanding black players in the major leagues. Hank Aaron led the Milwaukee Braves when they defeated the New York Yankees in the 1957 World Series, and his long career resounded in glory. On April 8, 1974, he did what had been considered impossible. He broke Babe Ruth's lifetime record of 714 home runs, and before he retired, Aaron hit 755 home runs, an amazing record that has never been broken.

Other outstanding black players in the 1950s were Willie Mays of the New York Giants, who for several years led the National League in home runs and stolen bases; the Chicago Cubs' shortstop Ernie Banks; pitcher Don Newcombe of the Brooklyn Dodgers, who in 1956 won the first Cy Young Award honoring the best major league pitcher; and Roy Campanella, another Brooklyn superstar, both as a hitter and a catcher. In 1958, Campanella was badly injured in an automobile accident that left him partly paralyzed and confined to a wheelchair.

The New York Giants and the Brooklyn Dodgers made news in another way in 1958. Both teams moved to the West Coast; the Giants to San Francisco and the Dodgers to Los Angeles. For the first time, major league baseball was now a transcontinental sport. While the Dodgers waited for their new stadium to be built, they drew large crowds to the Los Angeles Coliseum, a huge stadium used mainly for football games and track meets. Even playing in the almost cavernous coliseum, the Los Angeles Dodgers managed to win the 1959 World Series against the Chicago White Sox.

FOOTBALL

Bud Wilkinson's Oklahoma teams dominated college football in the 1950s. From 1953 to 1957, they won forty-seven straight games, establishing a record. Finally they were defeated by Notre Dame, 7–0.

Wilkinson's players had great respect for their successful coach. He said, "I always wanted to win, but I wanted to have fun, too. Once my players saw that winning was the most fun of all, they worked hard at it. I didn't drive them; I didn't have to. You can motivate players better with kind words than you can with a whip."[4]

Professional football in the fifties was much different than it is today. In that decade there was only the National Football League and no Super Bowl between the winners of two conferences. The American Football League did not begin until 1960, and it took several years before it achieved prominence. The first Super Bowl game between the top teams in the National Football League and the American Football League was played in 1967.

There was no dominant pro football team in the 1950s. The only teams that won more than one league championship were Baltimore (two), Detroit (three), and Cleveland (three). In 1957, the Cleveland Browns acquired a remarkable African-American fullback, Jim Brown. He averaged more than five yards every time he carried the ball and set an outstanding record by gaining 12,312 yards during his nine years at Cleveland.

On December 28, 1958, the New York Giants and the Baltimore Colts met for the league championship in what sportswriter Tex Maule called "the best football game ever played."[5] The Giants were leading, 17–14, but with only seven seconds left, the Colts' Steve Myhra kicked a field goal that tied the score.

This sent the game into overtime. Then Colt quarterback Johnny Unitas, starting on his team's 20-yard line, mixed short passes and runs to advance the ball up the field. On a wonderfully successful gamble, he threw a pass to tight end Jim Mutscheller, who caught it on the Giants' one-yard line. On the next play, fullback Alan Ameche plunged over the goal, giving the Colts a 23–17 victory.

This was the first championship pro football game broadcast coast to coast on television, and it had an estimated 50 million viewers. This single event more than any other transformed pro football into a major sports attraction, and beginning in the 1960s, more people watched the Super Bowl game than baseball's World Series.

BASKETBALL

Some of the college basketball teams that are still powerful today were also powerful in the 1950s. During that decade, Kentucky won two National Collegiate Athletic Association (NCAA) championship tournaments, while Kansas, North Carolina, and Indiana each won one.

The most sensational college star in the fifties was Bill Russell, a black player, who led the University of San Francisco to an incredible fifty-five straight victories and two national championships. Russell made such an impact on the game that the NCAA doubled the width of the foul line from 6 feet (2 m) to 12 feet (4m), and this became known as the "Russell rule."

Russell's coach, Phil Woolpert, said this new rule wasn't hurting his superstar. "As a matter of fact, this rule was made for him because he's as fast as he is big. He's so much the fastest of the big men that now he'll just leave them further behind."[6]

"I think it's a good rule," Russell declared. "It doesn't bother the tall players, but as for the fat ones and the slow ones, it kills them."[7] Actually, Bill Russell was only 6 feet 10 inches (208 cm) tall, but in his day that was considered a very tall basketball player.

Russell played in the 1956 Olympics and led the United States team to a gold medal. That year, the Boston Celtics traded two players to St. Louis for the rights to Russell, which sportswriter Joe Jares said was "probably the most important personnel deal in pro basketball's history."[8]

In professional basketball, the two most outstanding teams in the 1950s were the Minneapolis Lakers and the Boston Celtics. Led by George Mikan, Minneapolis won three straight titles early in the decade. Most of Mikan's basketball career occurred in the 1940s, but he continued to be a dominant player through the 1954 season. *Sport* magazine polled 123

Bill Russell of the Boston Celtics (#6) goes up against Wilt Chamberlain of the Philadelphia Warriors in a game in November 1961.

basketball coaches throughout the country, who named Mikan the greatest basketball player in the first half of the century.

After Mikan retired in 1954, a new professional basketball dynasty took shape in Boston. The superstars of the Celtics were Bob Cousy, Bill Sharman, Tom Heinsohn, and, of course, Bill Russell. Beginning with the 1958–1959 season, the Boston Celtics won eight pro championships in a row.

TRACK AND FIELD

On May 6, 1954, Roger Bannister, an English medical student, achieved what had been considered impossible. For generations, many track observers had believed that running 1 mile (1.6 km) in less than four minutes was beyond the reach of man. But on that date, Bannister ran a mile in an amazing 3:59.4 seconds. Some writers claimed that this was the greatest sports event of the century, and one, Arthur Daley, compared it to Sir Edmund Hillary's ascent of Mount Everest. "Two of mankind's supposedly unscalable peaks were surmounted at almost the same time," he declared enthusiastically.[9] However, forty-six days later, Australian John Landy ran almost a second and a half faster than Bannister's record.

The United States had more than its share of top-notch track and field athletes in the 1950s. In the 1952 Olympics at Helsinki, Finland, Bob Mathias won the decathlon for the second straight time. No other man in history had ever won the decathlon in two successive Olympic championships.

Other American gold medalists in the 1952 Olympics included Lindig Rimingo (100 meters, 10.4 seconds), Andy Stanfield (200 meters, 20.7 seconds), Mal Whitfield (800 meters, 1:49.2), and Harrison Dillard (110-meter hurdles, 13.7 seconds).

Two days after Bannister set the mile record, American Parry O'Brien became the first shot putter to throw the iron ball more than 60 feet (18 m). Traditionally, shot putters launched their efforts by standing at a right angle to the direction in which they would throw. But O'Brien introduced the practice of beginning with his back to the toeboard, thus pitting the force of his weight, strength, and agility into a 180-degree turn rather than the usual mere 90 degrees. This enabled O'Brien on May 8, 1954, to toss the iron ball 60 feet 5¼ inches (18 m). At the 1956 Olympics, he surpassed this mark, achieving a stunning 60 feet 11 inches.

In these 1956 Olympics, held at Melbourne, Australia, Americans won other gold medals. Charley Dumas high jumped 6 feet 11¼ inches (2 m), and later that year he soared over the bar at 7 feet 1/2 inch (2.1 m) to set a new world record. Al Oerter tossed the discus 184 feet 11 inches (56 m), and in 1962 he became the first man to throw the discus over 200 feet (61 m).

Bobby Morrow won three gold medals in the 1956 Olympics, running the 100 meters in 10.5 seconds and the 200 meters in 20.6 seconds. Glen Davis ran the 400-meter hurdles in 50.l seconds. Harold Connolly captured the hammer throw with a toss of 207 feet 3½ inches (63 m). Milton Campbell won the decathlon, and Patricia McCormick won gold medals in two diving events.

TENNIS

Pancho Gonzales was probably the best male tennis player in the 1950s, but women dominated the sport in that decade. At age sixteen, Maureen Connolly won the National Women's Singles Championship in 1951, becoming the youngest national tennis champion since 1901. "Little Mo" performed another remarkable feat in 1953. She won the Grand Slam of tennis, capturing the United States, Australian, French, and Wimbledon titles.

Althea Gibson also had a remarkable story in the fifties. Since she was African American, Gibson was handicapped in finding top-notch players to compete against because only a few tournaments then were open to blacks.

Finally, in 1950, she became the first African American allowed to compete in the U.S. Lawn Tennis Association's national championship. That year, Gibson was eliminated in the second round, but she kept trying. In 1957, at the age of thirty, she won both the United States and the Wimbledon crowns, thus ending the racial barrier in tennis. She repeated her double victory the following year.

GOLF

On February 2, 1949, Ben Hogan, the world's greatest golfer, was severely injured in an automobile accident. He suffered a double fracture of his pelvis and a broken collarbone, ankle-bone, and rib. A month after the crash, blood clots formed in both legs, and surgeons had to tie off the major veins in Hogan's legs. They doubted he would ever walk normally again, and certainly he would not play tournament golf.

Hogan, however, had indomitable courage and determination. Seventeen months after the accident, he won his second U.S. Open Tournament. In 1953, he became the first golfer to sweep the U.S. Open, the Masters, and the British Open in a single year.

Golf expert Herbert Warren Wind wrote that Hogan "was not only the outstanding golfer but the outstanding athlete of the postwar decade. He was perhaps the best golfer pound-for-pound who ever lived. . . . He expected perfection from himself and was always thinking in terms of the flawless shot, not the good shot. The green was not his target on his approaches, nor the quarter of the green around the pin. The flag was his target, and he drilled for it."[10]

Hogan continued playing golf until 1971, when at age fifty-eight, he participated in the last tournament of his distinguished career. In that event, his hands shook over putts, and on the fourth hole, he strained his knee. Leaving the course, he said to a friend, "Don't ever get old."[11]

After Hogan retired, Arnold Palmer became golf's next superstar. His first major victory was the 1954 Amateur Tournament. Palmer attained national prominence when he won the 1958 Masters Tournament at the famed course at Augusta, Georgia. Four times during his career, Palmer captured the Masters.

The nation's most famous golfer in the 1950s was not a professional player. He was Dwight D. Eisenhower, president of the United States. After Eisenhower moved into the White House, he played golf as often as he could. "People like to follow the leader," observed the operator of Washington, D.C.'s, public golf courses. "The papers keep talking golf. People start talking golf and then start playing it. I tell you, the President has really given the game a shot in the arm. . . . Ever since he went into the White House, all you hear is golf, golf, golf."[12]

Eisenhower usually shot in the middle 80s, and in 1956, the president who had suffered a heart attack won the Ben Hogan Trophy for being the player whose recovery from a physical ailment most inspired the community of golfers.

EPILOGUE

Because conformity seemed to be a predominant goal for many Americans in the 1950s, some people have called it the "bland decade." However, the fifties definitely were not bland or insignificant. It was a decade filled with events and changes that helped in important ways to shape the America we live in today.

Far from bland, this was a decade of contrasts. Americans enjoyed the security of prosperity under a strong economy. Yet the specters of Communism and the Korean and Cold wars haunted them. Women left the workforce to focus on home and family, signaling a return to a more traditional way of life. But important gains in civil rights for African Americans, the establishment of suburbs, the widespread popularity of television, and exciting new developments in entertainment made sure that life would never be the same as it had been at the dawn of the 1950s.

What was the legacy of the fifties? This question can be answered by considering the numerous ways in which American society evolved in those years. The impact of the sweeping changes that occurred in that decade, which still resonates today, lets us make the argument that the 1950s was one of the most pivotal periods in American history.

1950 The Korean War begins when North Korea attacks South Korea.
Chinese Communists attack UN forces in Korea.
President Harry Truman orders production of the hydrogen bomb.
Senator Joseph McCarthy starts his campaign against American Communists.
Alger Hiss is convicted of perjury.
Kefauver crime hearings begin on television.
Millions of Americans begin moving to the suburbs.

1951 General Douglas MacArthur is relieved of his command in the Korean War.
Julius and Ethel Rosenberg are sentenced to death on espionage charges.
Television replaces movies as the most popular form of entertainment.
I Love Lucy and Edward R. Murrow's *See It Now* debut on television.
Marlon Brando stars in the film *A Streetcar Named Desire*.
New York Giants defeat Brooklyn Dodgers as a result of Bobby Thomson's ninth-inning home run.

1952 The United States explodes the first hydrogen bomb.
Richard Nixon gives his famous "Checkers" speech.
Republican Dwight Eisenhower defeats Democrat Adlai Stevenson in the presidential election.
Bob Mathias becomes the first man to win the decathlon in two successive Olympic Games.
Gary Cooper stars in *High Noon*, perhaps the best Western movie ever made.

1953 An armistice ending the Korean War is signed at Panmunjom.
The Soviet Union tests its first hydrogen bomb.
Marilyn Monroe becomes the decade's leading sex symbol.
Oklahoma's football team begins a record streak of winning forty-seven straight games.

Maureen Connolly wins the Grand Slam in tennis, capturing four major singles titles.
Ben Hogan is the first golfer to win the U.S. Open, Masters, and British Open in one year.

1954   The Supreme Court votes to end segregation of black students in schools.
Senator McCarthy clashes with the U.S. Army, which leads to his downfall.
The navy launches the *Nautilus*, the first atomic-powered submarine.
Dr. Jonas Salk discovers the polio vaccine.
Ernest Hemingway wins the Nobel Prize for literature for *The Old Man and the Sea*.
Roger Bannister becomes the first man to run the mile in less than four minutes.
Shot-putter Parry O'Brien is the first man to toss the iron ball more than 60 feet (18 m).

1955   President Eisenhower suffers a heart attack.
Inspired by Rosa Parks, the Montgomery bus boycott begins.
Marian Anderson is the first black singer to play a leading role at the Metropolitan Opera.
The popular Western *Gunsmoke* debuts on television.
James Dean stars in three films and dies shortly after the last one.
Bill Russell leads San Francisco University's basketball team to fifty-five straight wins.
Men begin wearing pink shirts and pink striped or polka-dot ties.

1956   President Eisenhower defeats Stevenson again, winning a second term in the White House.
The United States opposes the war in the Suez Canal zone launched by three of its allies.
The National Defense Highway Act provides for building 41,000 miles (66,000 km) of freeways.
Singer Elvis Presley becomes an overnight sensation.
My Fair Lady, the biggest single musical hit of the decade, opens on Broadway.
Yankee Don Larsen pitches a World Series perfect game.
Dodger Don Newcombe wins the first Cy Young Award for the best major league pitcher.

1957
The Soviets' *Sputnik* is the first satellite to orbit Earth.
Eisenhower sends troops to end segregation at Little Rock High School.
The spectacular musical *West Side Story* opens on Broadway.
Jack Kerouac's *On the Road* is published, fueling the Beat Generation.
Althea Gibson ends the racial barrier in tennis, winning both the U.S. and Wimbledon crowns.

1958
The Eisenhower Doctrine is applied when U.S. troops are sent to Lebanon.
The United States enters the space race when *Explorer* is launched into orbit.
Commercial jet planes are introduced.
Hula hoops become a national fad for youngsters.
Boris Pasternak's *Doctor Zhivago* is published and sells 500,000 copies.
Van Cliburn wins first place in the International Tchaikovsky Piano Competition.
The New York Giants move to San Francisco, and the Brooklyn Dodgers to Los Angeles.
The Baltimore Colts' win over the New York Giants makes pro football a major sport.

1959
Fidel Castro seizes Cuba and becomes a Communist enemy of the United States.
The St. Lawrence Seaway is completed.
Hawaii and Alaska become states.
Soviet Premier Nikita Khrushchev visits the United States.
The television quiz show scandals are exposed.
The Cinemascope epic *Ben Hur* becomes a huge success.
The Sound of Music is the decade's last great musical stage show.
Frank Lloyd Wright's Guggenheim Museum opens in New York City.

SOURCE NOTES

Prologue

1. Joseph C. Goulden, *The Best Years: 1945–1950* (New York: Atheneum, 1976), p. 19.
2. Walter LaFeber, *The American Age: United States Foreign Policy at Home and Abroad Since 1750* (New York: Norton, 1989), p. 446.
3. David Halberstam, *The Fifties* (New York: Fawcett Columbine, 1993), p. 26.

Chapter One

1. William Manchester, *The Glory and the Dream: A Narrative History of America, 1932–1972*, Vol. 1 (Boston: Little, Brown, 1974), p. 653.
2. John Toland, *In Mortal Combat: Korea, 1950–1953* (New York: Morrow, 1991), p. 19.
3. Ibid., p. 37.
4. Manchester, p. 654.
5. John Whiteclay Chambers II, ed., *The Oxford Companion to American Military History* (New York: Oxford University Press, 1999), p. 369.
6. Manchester, p. 663.
7. Stuart A. Kallen, ed., *The 1950s* (San Diego, CA: Greenhaven Press, 2000), p. 48.
8. David Halberstam, *The Fifties* (New York: Fawcett Columbine, 1993), p. 110.
9. Editors, *This Fabulous Century: 1950* (New York: Time-Life Books, 1970), p. 38.
10. Ibid.
11. Ibid.
12. Toland, pp. 437–438.

Chapter Two

1. Douglas T. Miller and Marion Nowak, *The Fifties: The Way We Really Were* (New York: Doubleday, 1975), p. 27.
2. Jeremy Isaacs and Taylor Downing, *Cold War: An Illustrated History, 1945–1991* (Boston: Little, Brown, 1998), p. 113.
3. Miller and Nowak, p. 21.
4. Ibid., p. 22.

5. Ibid., pp. 28–29.
6. Eric F. Goldman, *The Crucial Decade and After: America, 1945–1960* (New York: Random House, 1960), p. 141.
7. Editors, *The American Dream: The 50s* (Alexandria, VA: Time-Life Books, 1998), p. 80.
8. Goldman, p. 142.
9. Editors, *This Fabulous Century: 1950* (New York: Time-Life Books, 1970), pp. 117–118.
10. Lisle A. Rose, *The Cold War Comes to Main Street: America in 1950* (Lawrence: University Press of Kansas, 1999), p. 154.
11. Ibid., p.157.
12. Editors, *This Fabulous Century*, p. 119.
13. Ibid., p. 13.

Chapter Three

1. David Halberstam, *The Fifties* (New York: Fawcett Columbine, 1993), pp. 209–210.
2. Michael Barone, *Our Country: The Shaping of America from Roosevelt to Reagan* (New York: The Free Press, 1990), p. 249.
3. Editors, *National Party Conventions, 1831–1992* (Washington, D.C.: Congressional Quarterly, 1995), p. 97.
4. Paul F. Boller Jr., *Presidential Campaigns* (New York: Oxford University Press, 1984), p. 281.
5. Gil Troy, *See How They Ran: The Changing Role of the Presidential Candidate* (Cambridge, MA: Harvard University Press, 1996), p. 197.
6. Eugene H. Roseboom and Alfred E. Eckles Jr., *A History of Presidential Elections* (New York: Macmillan, 1979), p. 224.
7. Editors, *National Party Conventions*, p. 99.
8. Albert M. Schlesinger Jr., ed., *Running for President: The Candidates and Their Images*, Vol. 2 (New York: Simon and Schuster, 1994), p. 265.
9. Ibid., p. 261.
10. Boller, pp. 283–284.
11. Edmund Lindop, *All About Republicans* (Hillside, NJ: Enslow, 1985), p. 69.
12. Boller, p. 284.
13. Lindop, p. 70.
14. Boller, p. 291.

Chapter Four

1. Jethro K. Lieberman, *The Evolving Constitution* (New York: Random House, 1992), p. 380.

2. Ibid., p. 381.
3. Ibid.
4. David Halberstam, *The Fifties* (New York: Fawcett Columbine, 1993), p. 416.
5. William Manchester, *The Glory and the Dream: A Narrative History of America, 1932–1972,* Vol. 2 (Boston: Little, Brown, 1973), p. 900.
6. Ibid., pp. 901-902.
7. Halberstam, p. 674.
8. Manchester, p. 984.
9. James MacGregor Burns, *The Crosswinds of Freedom* (New York: Knopf, 1989), pp. 348–349.
10. Harold Evans, *The American Century* (New York: Knopf, 1998), p. 472.
11. Ibid.
12. Halberstam, p. 556.

Chapter Five

1. Editors, *This Fabulous Century: 1950* (New York: Time-Life Books, 1970), p. 27.
2. Ibid.
3. Stuart A. Kallen, ed., *The 1950s* (San Diego, CA: Greenhaven Press, 2000), p. 92.
4. Warren I. Cohen, *America in the Age of Soviet Power, 1945–1991* (New York: Cambridge University Press, 1993), p. 89.
5. John Whiteclay Chambers II, ed., *The Oxford Companion to American Military History* (New York: Oxford University Press, 1999), p. 43.
6. Cohen, p. 95.
7. Jeremy Isaacs and Taylor Downing, *Cold War: An Illustrated History, 1945–1991* (Boston: Little, Brown, 1998), p. 139.
8. Isaacs and Downing, p. 155.
9. Ibid., p. 159
10. Alan Palmer, *Dictionary of 20th Century History* (New York: Facts on File, 1979), p. 351.
11. Edmund Lindop, *Cuba* (Danbury, CT: Franklin Watts, 1980), p. 26.

Chapter Six

1. Harold Evans, *The American Century* (New York: Knopf, 1998), p. 435.
2. Douglas T. Miller and Marion Nowak, *The Fifties: The Way We Really Were* (New York: Doubleday, 1975), p. 132.

3. William Manchester, *The Glory and the Dream: A Narrative History of America, 1932–1972*, Vol. 1 (Boston: Little, Brown, 1973), p. 527.
4. David Halberstam, *The Fifties* (New York: Fawcett Columbine, 1993), p. 137.
5. Manchester, p. 528.
6. Editors, *The American Dream: The 50s* (Alexandria, VA: Time-Life Books, 1998), p. 53.
7. Miller and Nowak, p. 138.

Chapter Seven

1. David Halberstam, *The Fifties* (New York: Fawcett Columbine, 1993), p. 185.
2. Ibid., p. 475.
3. *Newsweek*, January 19, 1953, p. 21.
4. Editors, *The American Dream: The 50s* (Alexandria, VA: Time-Life Books, 1998), p. 171.
5. Ibid.
6. Editors, *This Fabulous Century: 1950* (New York: Time-Life Books, 1970), p. 263.
7. Douglas T. Miller and Marion Nowak, *The Fifties: The Way We Really Were* (New York: Doubleday, 1975), p. 351.
8. William Manchester, *The Glory and the Dream: A Narrative History of America, 1932–1972*, Vol. 2 (Boston: Little, Brown, 1973), pp. 1041–1042.
9. Editors, *This Fabulous Century*, p. 269.

Chapter Eight

1. *Smithsonian*, March 1, 2001, p. 101.
2. Douglas T. Miller and Marion Nowak, *The Fifties: The Way We Really Were* (New York: Doubleday, 1975), p. 317.
3. Editors, *The American Dream: The 50s* (Alexandria, VA: Time-Life Books, 1998), p. 36.
4. Richard Griffith and Arthur Mayer, *The Movies* (New York: Bonanza Books, 1957), p. 66.
5. Ibid.
6. Editors, *Rock and Roll Generation: Teen Life in the 50s* (Alexandria, VA: Time-Life Books, 1998), p. 66
7. Ibid., p. 44.
8. Ibid.
9. David Halberstam, *The Fifties* (New York: Fawcett Columbine, 1993), p. 479.
10. Editors, *The American Dream*, p. 134.

Chapter Nine

1. Geoffrey C. Ward, *Baseball: An Illustrated History* (New York: Knopf, 1994), p. 324.
2. Ibid.
3. Editors, *The American Dream: The 50s* (Alexandria, VA: Time-Life Books, 1998), p. 177.
4. Wells Twombly, *200 Years of Sport in America: A Pageant of a Nation at Play* (New York: McGraw-Hill, 1976), p. 270.
5. Ibid., p. 245.
6. Joe Jares, *Basketball: The American Game* (Chicago, IL: Follett, 1971), p. 68.
7. Ibid.
8. Ibid., p. 209.
9. Twombly, p. 223.
10. Ibid., p. 240.
11. Ibid.
12. Edmund Lindop and Joseph Jares, *White House Sportsmen* (Boston: Houghton Mifflin, 1964), p. 94.

FURTHER READING

Ambrose, Stephen. *Eisenhower: The President.* New York: Simon and Schuster, 1984.

Blair, Clay. *The Forgotten War: America in Korea, 1950–1953.* New York: New York Times Books, 1987.

Boyer, Paul. *By the Bomb's Early Light: American Thought and Culture at the Dawn of the Atomic Age.* New York: Pantheon, 1985.

Clarke, Arthur, ed. *The Coming of the Space Age.* New York: Meredith Press, 1967.

Cohen, Daniel. *Joseph McCarthy: The Misuse of Political Power.* Brookfield, CT.: Millbrook, 1996.

Daly, Dan, and Bob O'Donnell. *The Pro Football Chronicle.* New York: Collier Books, 1990.

Dudley, Mark E. *Brown v. Board of Education: School Desegregation.* Brookfield, CT.: Millbrook, 1994.

Editors. *The American Dream: The 50s.* Alexandria, VA.: Time-Life Books, 1998.

Editors. *Rock and Roll Generation: Teen Life in the 50s.* Alexandria, VA: Time-Life Books, 1998.

Garraty, John A., ed. *The Young Reader's Companion to American History.* Boston: Houghton Mifflin, 1994.

Gordon, Lois, and Alan Gordon. *American Chronicle: Six Decades in American Life, 1920–1980.* New York: Atheneum, 1987.

Halberstam, David. *The Fifties.* New York: Fawcett Columbine, 1993.

Harvey, Brett. *The Fifties: A Woman's Oral History.* New York: HarperCollins, 1993.

Isaacs, Jeremy, and Taylor Downing, *Cold War: An Illustrated History, 1945–1991.* Boston: Little, Brown, 1998.

Jares, Joe. *Basketball: The American Game.* Chicago: Follett, 1971.

Kahn, Roger. *The Era: 1947–1957, When the Yankees, the Giants, and the Dodgers Ruled the World.* New York: Tickner and Fields, 1993.

Kallen, Stuart A., ed. *The 1950s.* San Diego, CA: Greenhaven Press, 2000.

Layman, Richard, ed. *American Decades: 1950–1959*. Detroit, MI: Gale Research, 1994.

Lewis, Peter, *The Fifties*. New York: Lippincott, 1978.

MacDonald, J. Fred. *One Nation Under Television*. New York: Pantheon, 1990.

Manchester, William. *The Glory and the Dream: A Narrative History of America, 1932–1972*. Boston: Little, Brown, 1973.

Manso, Peter. *Brando: The Biography*. New York: Hyperion, 1994.

McCullough, David. *Truman*. New York: Simon and Schuster, 1992.

McKeever, Porter. *Adlai Stevenson: His Life and Legacy*. New York: Morrow, 1989.

Miller, Douglas T., and Marion Nowak. *The Fifties: The Way We Really Were*. New York: Doubleday, 1977.

Morella, Joe, and Edward Z. Epstein. *Forever Lucy: The Life of Lucille Ball*. New York: Carol Publishing Group, 1986.

Moss, Norman. *Men Who Play God: The Story of the H-bomb and How the World Came to Live With It*. New York: Harper and Row, 1968.

Oates, Stephen B. *Let the Trumpet Sound: The Life of Martin Luther King, Jr.* New York: Harper and Row, 1982.

Parks, Rosa, and Gregory J. Reed. *Quiet Strength*. Grand Rapids, MI: Zondervan, 1994.

Quain, Kevin, ed. *The Elvis Reader*. New York: St. Martin's Press, 1992.

Solomon, Deborah. *Jackson Pollock*. New York: Simon and Schuster, 1987.

Stones, Barbara. *America Goes to the Movies*. North Hollywood, CA: National Association of Theater Owners, 1993.

Toland, John. *In Mortal Combat: Korea: 1950–1953*. New York: Morrow, 1991.

Twombly, Wells. *200 Years of Sport in America: A Pageant of a Nation at Play*. New York: McGraw-Hill, 1976.

Ward, Ed, Geoffrey Stokes, and Ken Tucker. *Rock of Ages: The Rolling Stone History of Rock and Roll*. New York: Simon and Schuster, 1986.

Ward, Geoffrey, C. *Baseball: An Illustrated History*. New York: Knopf, 1994.